Vikings

The History of the Vikings
Book 1

Vikings

The History of the Vikings, Volume 1

History Nerds

Published by History Nerds, 2022.

VIKINGS

First edition. November 2, 2022.

Copyright © 2022 History Nerds.

ISBN: 979-8215662915

Written by History Nerds.

Also by History Nerds

Celtic History
Ireland

Great Wars of the World
World War 1
World War 2
The Napoleonic Wars: One Shot at Glory
The Serbian Revolution: 1804-1835
Peace Won by the Saber: The Crimean War, 1853-1856
The Wars of the Roses

Irish Heroes
Grace O'Malley: The Pirate Queen of Ireland
William Butler Yeats: Nobel Prize Winning Poet
Scáthach
Finn McCool

The History of the Vikings

Vikings
Longships on Restless Seas

The Rise and Fall of Empires
Rome: The Rise and Fall

Standalone
The History of the United Kingdom
The History of Ireland
The History of America
Stalin
The Fiery Maelstrom of Freedom
The History of Scotland
Robert the Bruce
William Wallace: Scotland's Great Freedom Fighter
The History of Wales

Table of Contents

Introduction

Few are those that have not heard of the fearsome Vikings and their daring exploits. These Northern seafarers, the scourge of the Middle Ages, left their mark on the world's history in a grand fashion. Courageous, defiant, and driven by the desire for exploration, the Norsemen were the most feared of all Medieval conquerors. Many thought them invincible, and they held many struggling Christian nations in their sway. From Scotland, England, France, and Ireland, down to the shores of Spain and the Baltic, the Vikings left their undeniable mark. Brutal conquest was not the only tool of their trade: these men were able seafarers and great explorers. Vikings discovered and established colonies in the Faroe Islands, Iceland, Greenland, and North America. Many agree that they were the first to set foot in the land we know today as Canada. All in all, the Vikings hold a vital role in the history of the world. Who knows how our world would look today if it weren't for these grand Norsemen?

It was June 8th, AD 793, on Lindisfarne, an island off England's northeastern coast. For the pious monks of the island's monastery, the day dawned just like any other. Nothing suggested extraordinary events. On this morning, history unraveled one of its most significant and cardinal events, the arrival of the Vikings. From the gloom of the morning mists, piercing the thin veil of sea foam, dragonheads emerged. They were the decorated prows of Viking ships laden with eager and fierce warriors from the North. Lindisfarne monastery was viciously sacked: the helpless monks had never before experienced such wanton violence. The Norsemen were there to raid and attain riches by any means possible. This they did - the monks were slain without mercy, offering no resistance, and their rich monastery gifts and treasures were taken away. It was a shocking event that took the Christian world by surprise. The Anglo-Saxon Kingdoms of England were taken unawares. They had no clue of these sea raiders from the

North nor knew their motives for such a brutal assault. It was a surprisingly easy raid for the Vikings, who wanted *more*. So it is that AD 793 is seen as the beginning of the great Viking Age, an era that would change the flow of Medieval Europe from the ground up. This is the story of the *Vikings*.

Chapter I - The Earliest Viking Age and the Assault on Lindisfarne

On the Anglo-Saxon holy island of Lindisfarne, June 8th, AD 793, dawned much like all the others. Nothing indicated that an epic event would unfold that very day. Lindisfarne was the home of Lindisfarne Priory, a revered early medieval Anglo-Saxon monastery founded in AD 634 by Saint Aidan, a holy Irish monk. It was an important religious site, one of the foremost in Anglo-Saxon England, and the seat of Christian evangelism in the North of England. Above all, it was a rich monastery by AD 793, filled with relics and treasures donated by the nobles and kings of Northumbria. For decades and decades, the monastery enjoyed peace and prosperity, its monks entirely devoted to the ascetic and reserved worship of Christ. Nothing could prepare these pious men for what would happen on June 8th. On that morning, the votive and decorated dragon heads emerged from the early morning mist - prows of swift and vicious Viking longships. The Norsemen, hitherto little-known to the majority of early medieval Europe, have decided to seek out new lands to settle and raid, looking beyond the North Sea for their new victims. They discovered the holy site at Lindisfarne and knew the gods were on their side. Finding the Christian monastery, the Viking seafarers knew it was a powerful prize. They descended upon the monks, realizing they did not offer any resistance. A real massacre occurred, a raid of a truly infamous character. The medieval Anglo-Saxon chronicle mentions this dreadful event:

"Her wæron reðe forebecna cumene ofer Norðhymbra land, 7 þæt folc earmlic bregdon, þæt wæron ormete þodenas 7 ligrescas, 7 fyrenne dracan wæron gesewene on þam lifte fleogende. Þam tacnum sona fyligde mycel hunger, 7 litel æfter þam, þæs ilcan geares on .vi. Idus Ianuarii, earmlice

hæþenra manna hergunc adilegode Godes cyrican in Lindisfarnaee þurh hreaflac 7 mansliht"
Translated:
"In this year, fierce, foreboding omens came over the land of the Northumbrians, and the wretched people shook; there were excessive whirlwinds, lightning, and fiery dragons were seen flying in the sky. These signs were followed by great famine, and a little after those, that same year on 6th ides of January, the ravaging of wretched heathen men destroyed God's church at Lindisfarne."

The given date of January 6th is seen as a scribe's error, and the 8th of June is the accepted date when there would undoubtedly have been better sailing weather beneficial to the Vikings. Another contemporary account, made by a Northumbrian scholar present at the esteemed court of Charlemagne, writes of the shocking event:

"Never before has such terror appeared in Britain as we have now suffered from a pagan race ... The heathens poured out the blood of saints around the altar and trampled on the bodies of saints in the temple of God, like dung in the streets."

The fierce pagan Vikings showed no mercy for the pious Christian monks. Clergymen and scribes were cut to pieces, massacred, drowned in the sea as sacrificial offerings, and murdered brutally. Some were taken as slaves, later to be sold in the slave markets of the North. Ancient relics and rich items of gold and silver were taken as war booty. They were likely welcomed as a considerable difference from the poor plunder the Vikings acquired up to that point in remote and more impoverished lands. Thus, the Vikings, those fierce Norsemen, introduced themselves to the general populace of early medieval Europe. The attack on the holy island of Lindisfarne came as a brutal shock for the entire Christian world. It spread throughout Europe, whose inhabitants could scarcely believe that a peaceful monastery could have been so brutally plundered and its monks massacred. The news of the pagan "Norsemen," as they were generally called, spread like wildfire, and fear was at once instilled in the bones of pious civilians. Who were they? What was their intent, and why have they harbored such wanton hate for the Christians? These questions arose quickly and would be answered over the following decades and centuries in what would later be called the Viking Age - an era of European history that was opened in AD 793, with the attack on Lindisfarne: the beating heart of Christianity in Anglo-Saxon England.

The attack in AD 793 on Lindisfarne Abbey was likely not the first such Viking encounter. The Norsemen arrived on the shores of England in years prior, perhaps as early as AD 750. However, there is no specific evidence or written accounts of these early Viking arrivals, and we cannot say they were violent. One account reports that four years before Lindisfarne, a fleet of three Viking ships beached in Weymouth Bay, but no violence likely occurred. Scribes would undoubtedly have mentioned it if it was a violent and massive raid. The AD 793 attack at the abbey on Lindisfarne was unprecedented. The massacre took the Anglo-Saxon society unawares and was so brutal and violent that it stunned the Christian world. So ferocious were the Norse raiders that the Christian monks believed them to be the creatures of doomsday. The event was described as "the day of God's judgment upon the world." Subsequently, the Vikings were feared more than anything. The Christian monks popularly penned their short prayer: "A furore Normannorum Libera nos, Domine." *Translated - "Free us from the fury of the Northmen, Lord."*

Why were the Vikings such a significant threat to the early medieval realms of Europe? To answer this question, we first focus on Anglo-Saxon England, arguably the first Viking target. Around AD 793, the kingdoms of the Anglo-Saxons were primarily occupied by their internal affairs. Ever since the Angles, the Jutes, and the Saxons swept over the Brythonic realms in the 500s AD, the islands were plunged into internal conflicts. The Anglo-Saxon kingdoms of Mercia,

Northumbria, Wessex, and others - all warred between themselves but also came into conflict with the Brythonic Welsh and Cornish, the Picts in the North, and the Gaels as well. These internal conflicts left the British isles vulnerable primarily to attacks from outside, from the seas. Another contributing factor to their fear of the Vikings was their new Christian faith. After arriving in the British Isles, the ferocious Anglo-Saxon pagans were quickly assimilated into a growing Christian society. The followers of Christ preached a different worldview, distanced from the "rugged" and "barbaric" pagan beliefs. In no time, the Anglo-Saxon leaders became akin to other great monarchs of Europe - patrons of monasteries and the clergy, preachers of peace and supporters of ascetic monasticism. By the time of the Vikings, they were so separated from their distant pagan past that they were wholly taken unawares by the ferocity of the pagan Northerners.

The Vikings appeared "out of the blue," literally and metaphorically. No one expected such brutal raiding parties to descend from the north and to lay waste to peaceful Christian communities, but they did. One question needs to be addressed: what spurred the Vikings to begin raiding and pillaging in the first place? The Scandinavians indeed began a remarkable expansion from the 8th to 11th centuries. Firstly, we must agree that life in the Scandinavian lands was becoming markedly different than in the distant past, in the Nordic Bronze Age. By the AD 800s, there appears to have been a centralized rule in the Jutland Peninsula in modern Denmark. Could that have spurred wild Viking parties to set sail? Answering this question is difficult, as no single answer can be given. Instead, scholars put forward several possible theories explaining the sudden appearance of Viking raiding parties. Let's go over them in detail.

The first theory that is put forward regards demographics in Scandinavia. Some scholars say that the Vikings were driven to the seas because of a lack of women, which was caused by widespread female infanticide - i.e., the deliberate murder of newborn female babies.

However, this theory has since been disregarded as somewhat illogical. The other part of the demographic theory is the opposite: overpopulation caused the Vikings to raid. A steep rise in the population numbers meant that the available agricultural capacities in Scandinavia were depleted. The younger sons, unable to inherit any land for themselves, were forced to seek new lands to settle and farm outside the boundaries of their homeland. In the society of this era, younger sons who had no land to inherit were left with no status and few prospects in life. Many of these "lesser sons" were thus keen to go raiding and wage war, seeking better fortunes. Piracy and raiding were, of course, a quick path toward great material wealth. With that, a young man could quickly get enough money to settle and purchase his own land. A life of adventure, war, and plunder attracted many a restless young warrior in Scandinavia. In time, these war parties began looking beyond the Scandinavian boundaries to the Baltic shores, northern Europe, and eventually to Britain.

The next theory is economic. If we were to put it in simpler terms, we could call it the "greedy" theory. It has to deal with money. It is a well-known fact that the 8th century was particularly prosperous across Europe. Trade routes were expanded, the Islamic world grew, and wealthier urban centers began to prosper. These wealthy cities boomed, especially in Anglo-Saxon England and elsewhere in North-Central Europe. Naturally, Vikings were drawn toward them. However, it was easier for them to raid and increase their wealth.

There is also the proposed theory that internal conflicts and the pressures on their borders caused the Vikings to set sail and seek new lands to plunder. The shores of the Baltic were not rich in particular, and the area of northwest Germany and central Europe were out of bounds. The Franks were well-organized and well-defended and placed increased pressure on the borders of the Jutland Peninsula. Furthermore, the growth of centralized rule within the Scandinavian realms, as we mentioned, led to increased tensions and conflicts within the Viking world. The raiders and those in conflict with the Viking rulers quickly looked abroad for new lands to settle or pillage. Anglo-Saxon England, and the British Isles as a whole, were a ripe prize to take. They were immersed in their new Christian world and occupied with internal struggles. After that initial experience at Lindisfarne, the Vikings realized that waging war on the English would be no trouble.

Of course, there was also the immense yawning gap between Germanic Paganism and Christianity. It was a gap that could never have been mended, and great animosity existed between these religions. The Vikings possessed a great hatred for the Christian faith, which attempted to usurp their traditions and traditional way of life and demonize their ancient gods and goddesses. Not at all surprisingly, the Viking attack on Lindisfarne in AD 793 roughly coincides with the Saxon Wars, waged by the Frankish and Lombard Christian King, Charlemagne. This was a series of brutal campaigns, 18 in total, lasting from AD 772 to 804. In simplest terms, it was Charlemagne's Christian war against the Pagan Saxons in Northwest Germany and their forcible conversion to the Christian religion. Together with the neighboring Polabian Slavs, the pagan Saxons suffered greatly at the hands of the Christian Franks. Many massacres were recorded, and the forcible conversion of innocent common folk. These increased pressures on the Germanic Pagans likely caused the Vikings to seek new lands to settle outside Charlemagne's reach. After all, the Danish Vikings, dwelling on the Jutland Peninsula, were directly bordered by the Saxons, so recently devastated. Should it then be surprising that the Vikings quickly decided to seek new lands to the West, seeing how their neighbors fared? Finding them thoroughly Christian, they decided to give wings to all their wrath.

There is a standard theory that suggests it was a technological improvement, above all, that allowed the Vikings to set sail to the distant Western lands. Up to that point, their seafaring practices were reserved only for the "local" waters - Skagerak, Kattegat, the Baltic Sea, and the adjacent gulfs. New innovations possibly allowed them to cover greater distances at sea, use larger sails, navigate without the sun, and sail for 24 hours. This allowed for new explorations towards the West, at which point they chanced upon the unsuspecting British Isles. In the end, whichever theory we accept, one thing remains certain: the Vikings set sail, and this ushered Europe into a wholly new era, whose destiny was now dictated by the rhythmic beat of northern oars.

Chapter II - The Fight Against the Anglo-Saxons

Before we delve deep into the history of the Vikings and the era they dominated, we should first interest ourselves in their unique identity. Who exactly were the Vikings? Was this their real name? This is the first issue we must tackle; after all, much knowledge can be hidden in a word. The most straightforward truth is that the Vikings did not call themselves that. The term "Viking" was used throughout the Middle Ages to denote the seafaring pirates from the North. This, however, was the common name used by the people that the Vikings oppressed. What is the meaning of it? The word "Viking" means simply "a pirate." It is an Old Norse word stemming from the words "vikja" (to ambush) and "vik" (bay). Translated, it means "bay-lurker" or "bay-pirate." In ancient times, pirates of Scandinavian society would hide their swift and maneuverable boats in narrow fjords, lagoons, and canyons. From there, they would swiftly descend and ambush trading ships and seafaring travelers.

By the early medieval period, "to go Viking" meant to go on a raiding party. One quote states, "All Vikings were Norse, but not all Norse were Vikings, only those that went raiding." Still, the word stuck throughout Europe, and the Norsemen became known as the Vikings, the definition of their trade. They mostly did not call themselves such, but likely used tribal and ethnic designations (Danes, Norwegians, or Swedes) and commonly called themselves Northmen or Eastman, depending on where they were. The historian David Wilson sums it up nicely:

"One of the problems facing any serious writer dealing with the Viking Age concerns the usage of the term 'Viking' itself, which I have used - if sparingly - in much of this book. The word 'Viking' did not come into general use in the English language until the middle of the nineteenth

Century - at about the same time it was introduced into serious academic literature in Scandinavia - and has since changed its meaning and been much abused. It must, however, be accepted that the term is today used throughout the world as a descriptor of the peoples of Scandinavia in the period from the late eighth Century until the mid-eleventh Century. To the general public, however, it has apparently two meanings; both are respectable and hallowed in the English language by two centuries of usage. The first is in the sense of 'raider' or 'pirate,' the second in the sense of the activities of the Scandinavians outside their own country in that period. The latter meaning has given rise to the useful term 'the Viking Age.' Disregarding the ultimate philology of the word and the history of its use over the centuries, which has been much discussed, it is now in such everyday use by both specialists and non-specialists - however improperly - to describe the Scandinavians of the Viking Age that it is almost impossible to avoid its use in this generic sense. Although it is often appropriate and necessary to use such terms as 'Scandinavian' or 'Norse,' as I have done in this book, it is often simpler and less confusing to label something as 'Viking' rather than deal in scholastic circumlocution to placate purists, however, justified they may be in their arguments."

They could have arrived from a variety of places across Scandinavia. By the middle ages, many prosperous Viking towns existed across the north. Depending on the region, they were always ready to send new warring fleets. Some of the most important cities in Scandinavia during the Viking Age were Oslo, Kaupang, Sarpsborg, and Trondheim in Norway; Uppsala, Birka, Sigtuna, and others in Sweden; and Viborg, Aarhus, Ribe, Kaupmannahǫfn (Copenhagen), Hedeby, and others. It was from these and other cities that the Viking fleets set sail. However, it is important to note that not all Viking groups sailed in the same direction. Depending on where they lived, they would prefer the Western, Eastern, or even Southern routes. During this book, we shall detail these "routes" and the impact the Norsemen had on them. For now, we shall begin with the western direction, with the first contacts of the Vikings and the peoples of the British Isles.

We mentioned the attack on Lindisfarne as the first and most shocking Viking attack in the British Isles and Europe. However, it was not the first, but it was undoubtedly the most shocking. It isn't out of the question that even before AD 793, the Vikings, or the Northmen, were a known and feared threat to the Anglo-Saxons. Some sporadic encounters were more likely, but perhaps not as violent as the Lindisfarne raid. Either way, medieval documents and chronicles tell us that the first known and documented account of a Viking raid occurred a few years before Lindisfarne, in AD 789. This year, we are told, three Viking ships arrived from distant Hordaland, in modern Norway, and landed on the Isle of Portland, just off the southern coast of Wessex. The waves and their sails brought them to the British Isles, and their first intent was plunder and piracy. When spotted, the Vikings were quickly approached by one Beaduheard, a local Dorchester reeve, an official whose duty was to identify all new and foreign merchants entering the Kingdom of Wessex. He mistook the Vikings for traders and learned of his mistake the hard way since the Northmen replied to his inquiries by murdering him and all his men. Contemporary accounts described this event in several places, mentioning, amongst other things, that the reeve used an "authoritative" tone of voice and was murdered for it.

"(In 789) Here, Beorhtric took King Offa's daughter Eadburh. And in his days came first three ships from Hordaland: and then the reeve rode there and wanted to compel them to go to the king's town because he did not know who they were, and then they killed him. These were the first ships of the Danish men which sought out the land of the English race."

Even though the Anglo-Saxon Chronicle tells us that this was the first fleet of Norse ships that arrived in the British Isles, such encounters indeed occurred in the preceding months or years. They were unrecorded at the time and thus remain unknown to us. One piece of evidence can be traced to a letter written sometime between AD 790 and 792, penned by Alcuin and addressed to King Æthelred I of Northumbria. In this letter, Alcuin criticizes the English for "copying the fashions of pagans who menaced them with terror." This statement suggests that close encounters with the Norse existed, and a degree of cultural exchange also occurred. Of course, this also indicates that the Vikings knew a thing or two about the Anglo-Saxons and their lands and thus knew which targets to attack. In AD 793, they went for one of the most important ones, Lindisfarne. This prosperous monastery was thoroughly sacked and ravaged by a Viking raiding party on June 8th. As we mentioned, it was a shocking and bold assault on Christian Anglo-Saxon realms. Revolted, the Archbishop Alcuin of York writes of the event:

"Lo, it is nearly 350 years that we and our fathers have inhabited this most lovely land, and never before has such a terror appeared as we have now suffered from a pagan race, nor was it thought that such an inroad from the sea could be made. Behold the church of St Cuthbert spattered with the blood of the priests of God, despoiled of all its ornaments."

Once the Norsemen tasted the sweetness of such a bountiful plunder of gold and precious items, they were not eager to "call it a day." The following year, AD 794, they appeared out of the mist, sacking the Monkwearmouth-Jarrow Abbey near Lindisfarne. The pillage was equally devastating. However, it was not as simple as before. Some records state that the Vikings met with resistance at Jarrow, likely from the local magnates. Combat ensued, and some of the Norse leaders were killed. Subsequently, they escaped, and their ships beached at Tynemouth, where once more, they were assaulted and decimated by the local populace. For the Vikings, this was one of the first defeats on the shores of Anglo-Saxon Britain, and it was enough to deter them for some 40 years. During this period, no Viking fleets came to England, but they explored the coasts of Ireland and Scotland and only raided unprotected monasteries in England. It was becoming clear that the

Vikings sailed along the coast and that new raiding fleets arrived each year. Like wolves circling a herd of sheep, they prowled and assaulted unexpectedly, swiftly, and viciously.

The following year too, they appeared, in AD 795, when they attacked one of the cradles of Christianity in the British Isles, the famed Iona monastery off the west coast of Scotland. Its many riches were plundered. The Vikings would return to Iona on several occasions: in AD 802, 806, and 825, laying waste to it every time. In AD 825, the damage was near-final: 68 monks were massacred in the island's bay, almost the entire population. This caused the remaining monks to abandon the place and flee to the new Abbey of Kells in Ireland, seeking refuge. The sack of Iona was one of the significant blows to the Anglo-Saxons and cemented the Vikings' image as uncompromising and ruthless heathen raiders. Iona was the home of St. Columba, one of the first missionaries that spread Christianity through Scotland. The Vikings found it a lucrative target since they returned on several occasions. Not at all surprisingly, each new raid on Iona sent further shockwaves throughout Christian Europe. We can find contemporary accounts as far as the Carolingian Empire, which condemns and eulogizes the poor monks' massacres. Even more interestingly, modern archeology provides evidence of these Viking raids. In several warrior graves in Sweden and Norway, archeologists discovered lavish croziers, luxury items, and other riches that could be traced back to Iona. Plunder was in abundance, and raiding was a lucrative "business." For some, it was seen as a sure way of income, an "innocent" adventure that assured money throughout the year. Some records tell us that some Vikings, throughout the Viking Age, embarked on these raids in months when agricultural work was slow. Back in time to reap the harvest, and then off again to reap a different crop, the gold and silver type.

In many ways, the Vikings were like wolves. Once they tasted the blood of the Christian men, they wanted more, so they kept returning.

Every few years, when the weather and the funds permitted, new Viking fleets were raised and directed toward the shores of the British Isles. The first considerable Viking invasion that is documented occurred in AD 835. This year, the Norsemen assaulted the Isle of Sheppey, a part of the Kingdom of Wessex. This was the first significant assault on South England and would prove to be the stepstone for further invasions by the Danish Vikings. At Sheppey, vulnerable coastal monasteries were plundered, and their halls were used as headquarters for the Norse. Sheppey became one of their first permanent bases. They spent a winter on the isle and resumed their raids in springtime. The Isle of Sheppey would continue to suffer in subsequent decades. Next, the Norse sailed their longboats up the River Thames and assaulted the vulnerable Isle of Thanet. Smallish but still well-populated, Thanet also boasted several hamlets and monasteries, all of which were ravaged. By AD 851 and again in AD 854, the Norse spent their winters at Thanet, posing a significant threat to the surrounding Anglo-Saxons.

By this point, the Norse were a threat for more than 50 years, returning to pillage sporadically. However, during this period, they realized that the Anglo-Saxon realm had more to offer than just coastal raids. It offered land. Thus, the Norse changed their intentions for Britain: instead of simply looting it, they wanted to settle, farm the land and make a new home for themselves, away from Scandinavia. It took 50 years for the word to spread in Scandinavia. There were new lands to the West, many islands that were fertile and rich in gold and silver. For the economic situation in the Norse lands, this was the perfect solution. From AD 865 onwards, more extensive fleets came to the British shores with the clear intent to settle the lands. To do that meant one thing, war.

Viking colonization of Britain meant many changes. Culturally, the two civilizations were thoroughly different. First and foremost was religion—Christianity on one side and Norse Paganism on the other.

Then there were the social habits, cultures, language, clothing and diet, customs, traditions, and beliefs. Both of these civilizations were Germanic in origin, but still, they were different. That clash meant that peaceful coexistence would be challenging to achieve. Because of this, the Vikings began assembling a large enough army that could pose a significant threat to the Anglo-Saxons and would be strong enough to carve out their new realm. This army would become known as the Great Heathen Army, or Mycel Hæþen Here, as the Anglo-Saxons called it. This army resulted from several Viking chieftains banding together, understanding that once their fleets were assembled and directed in unison, their power would be much more significant. According to the near-contemporary Anglo-Saxon chronicle, this Great Viking Army was led by powerful Norse chiefs: Ivar the Boneless and Halfdan Ragnarsson. For Britain, this was a threat never before seen.

In AD 865, the massive Viking army landed on English coasts, ready for war. In that same year, they ravaged East Anglia and set their sights on York, a principal city of the Kingdom of Northumbria. Chronicles say that Ivar the Boneless was together with Ubbe, another key leader. The intentions are also mentioned: they were intent on avenging their father, a legendary chieftain Ragnar Lodbrok (Ragnar Shaggy-breeches), one of the most infamous of all Viking raiders whom the Anglo-Saxons torturously slew. However, no positive historic confirmations of this connection exist. Either way, the massive Norse army quickly achieved its goals and captured York in AD 866 without much trouble.

Desperate, the Northumbrians attempted to retake their principal city, and launched a counterattack that resulted in the Battle of York, fought on March 21st, AD 867. Ivar the Boneless and Ubba, at the head of their army, were assaulted by the Northumbrian leaders, Osbehrt and Ælla. The battle was a major Anglo-Saxon defeat: even though their army made it through the city walls, the fighting inside turned into a bloodbath. Many Anglo-Saxon warriors were slain, as were both Northumbrian leaders, Osbehrt and Ælla. Viking tradition states that Ivar and Ubbe captured Ælla alive and then "blood-eagled" him as a way of revenge for the death of their father. A blood eagle was a brutal execution reserved only for the worst offenders and enemies. However, other medieval accounts tell us that both Northumbrian leaders fell in the battle. Either way, York was now decisively Viking and was known to them as Jorvik. For the whole Anglo-Saxon realm, losing York had devastating consequences. It was one of the wealthiest trading centers in Britain and one of only two archiepiscopal sees. From there, the Norse gained a significant foothold for their further conquest of Britain.

In the meantime, the Great Heathen Army quickly replenished its losses, reinforced by another great Norse army led by a chieftain named Guthrum. They were quick to solidify their rule over the East Angles, placing puppet kings who would work in their favor. With their capitulation, the Norsemen now focused on the south of Britain, to the Kingdom of Wessex. Some scholars suggest that, since Wessex was the last of the Anglo-Saxon realms to stand against the Vikings, the latter were shrewd enough to isolate and deal with it last. In AD 870, reinforced by Guthrum's army, the Great Heathen Army arrived at the city of Reading on the banks of the Thames River. Over the following several months, the Norse fought nine battles with their enemies.

Now, accounts on this period might be a bit scarce, but what is certain is that not long after the clashes at Reading, the Great Heathen Army split: one part struck out into Wessex, likely led by Guthrum. What ensued from this invasion was the historic Battle of Englefield, fought on December 31st, AD 870, near Reading in Berkshire. At Englefield, a prowling Viking army was met in battle against Æthelwulf, Ealdorman of Berkshire. The clash was fierce, and one of the Norse leaders fell in battle, after which his army was repulsed and fled. It was a rare Norse defeat, but the West Saxon victory would prove short-lived.

Just four days later, the main Wessex army, led by King Ethelred himself and his brother, the future King Alfred the Great, assaulted the main encampment of the Danish Vikings at Reading. The Battle of Reading was fought on January 4th, AD 871. Although managing to kill many Danes on the city perimeter, the West Saxons were utterly defeated by a fierce Viking counterattack outside the city walls. Æthelwulf of Berkshire was slain in this battle, but Ethelred and Alfred both managed to flee with the tattered remnants of their army. Reading was not the last such clash, as new and fierce battles soon followed. The West Saxons regrouped, and just four days after Reading, they fought the Danes again in the famed Battle of Ashdown on January 8th, AD 871. A close-pitched battle, and one of the most violent in this period, Ashdown was a decisive Wessex victory attributed to the valiant command of young Alfred. The Norse suffered heavy losses, with many chieftains falling in battle. However, the morale boost of the West Saxon forces was short-lived. Two more battles were fought: the Battle of Basing, fought on January 22nd, AD 871; and the Battle of Meretun, fought on March 22nd, AD 871. Both were decisive Viking victories. The Anglo-Saxon Chronicle writes:

"King Æthelred and his brother Alfred fought against the army at Basing, and there the Danes had the victory. And two months later, King Æthelred and his brother Alfred fought against the army at Meretun, and they were in two divisions, and they put both to flight and were victorious far on into the day, and there was a great slaughter on both sides, and the Danes had possession of the battlefield. And Bishop Heahmund was killed there and many important men. And after this battle, a great summer army came to Reading. And afterwards, at Easter, King Æthelred died."

As the chronicle writes, King Ethelred died soon after Easter. His successor, King Alfred (to be called "the Great"), would prove to be a promising leader who would rise to do great deeds during his reign. First, he had to continue his conflict with the invading Danish Vikings.

Around this time, one of the prominent leaders of the Norse in Britain, Halfdan Ragnarsson, gradually begins "disappearing" from written records, as he presumably surrendered his lands in East Anglia and Northumbria to new waves of Danish invaders that arrived in AD 876. It could be that Halfdan was ousted by a new chieftain and went to Ireland to seize the throne of Dublin. Of course, we shall address the Viking invasion of Ireland separately and mention Halfdan again. Between AD 876 and 880, the Norse kept acquiring other lands within Mercia and East Anglia while fighting with King Alfred. All the while, the Danes seemed to be an insurmountable obstacle, nearly invincible in battle, to the point that Alfred was losing hope.

Early in King Alfred's reign, the Danes crushed the Saxons at the Battle of Wilton, where the King himself was present. Witnessing the defeat, Alfred was sure the Danes could not be driven out of his realms and Britain. Chronicles mentions that Alfred was thus forced to seek peace on terms now unknown to us. The Norse were likely paid a hefty sum to withdraw from Alfred's realm. However, the peace did not last long, as the conflict continued in the following years. In early AD 878, the Danes made a surprise attack on the Royal castle at Chippenham, where Alfred was staying with his retinue. Many Saxons were slain, and Alfred barely managed to flee with a ragtag band of supporters. From there, he fled eastwards, finally finding refuge in Somerset's remote moors and marshlands. Accounts tell us that he made a fortress in the marshes, at a place called Athelney ("Prince's Isle"), and from this stronghold continued to fight against the Danes. He recuperated and led a resistance force, gathering militias and supporters across the region.

By AD 880, most Anglo-Saxon Britain was under Danish occupation, and Wessex alone stood as a defiant barrier continuing the fight. Here we can draw a conceptualized map of Britain as it appeared around this time. The lands where the Danish Vikings held sway would later be called "Danelaw" and spread from Northumbria in the north all the way south to London, where it bordered Wessex. Danelaw was the part of Britain where the Danes established themselves as warriors, marauding bands, and settlers. The Vikings are reported to have plowed and supported themselves off the land, living as full-fledged settlers. The boundaries between these regions were "formalized" in AD 886 with the Treaty of Wedmore, signed between the Viking leaders from East Anglia and the ruler of Wessex. It was clear that the areas north and east of this boundary were influenced by Viking politics, while those south and west remained dominated by the Anglo-Saxons, in this case by Wessex and its dependencies.

After the temporary peace between Alfred and the Vikings, i.e., after the Wedmore treaty, the Wessex King could now focus on strengthening his realm, having learned some hard but valuable lessons during the war. He set about constructing a series of "burhs," or fortified towns, mainly along the borders and also started building a navy since his enemies were largely seafaring and sea-based. Alfred also organized a new-style militia system called the "fyrd," through which half of the entire peasant army was always in active service. To maintain the military and the new burhs, he created new taxation and a new conscription system known as Burghal Hidage. These latest moves proved to be a shrewd decision, as in AD 892, a new Viking fleet sailed over from the north, this time numbering 250 ships, a massive army. It arrived on the shores of Kent and was headquartered there, and soon bolstered with reinforcements of another 80 ships. This new Norse army continued to wage destructive war on Wessex, determined to break its resistance. However, this suddenly proved to be a greater challenge, all because of the new measures that Alfred put into action. Wessex was now a hard nut to crack, and the Vikings were not as successful as they had hoped. Even still, seeing that Wessex could not be easily overwhelmed, the Vikings gradually dispersed. Some settled alongside their compatriots in East Anglia and Northumbria, while others sailed elsewhere to pillage Ireland and the Isles or cross over to Normandy.

Even in the days after the reign of Alfred, his successors were fierce opponents of the Viking settlers in the so-called "Danelaw." His daughter Æthelflæd and her brother, Edward, the Elder, fought the Norse and gradually pushed back the Danelaw region boundaries. King Edward the Elder died in AD 924 and was succeeded by his son, Æthelstan. By AD 927, the latter managed to conquer Jorvik, better known as York, the last remaining Viking stronghold. Ambitious and spurred on by his victories, Æthelstan pushed north and invaded Scotland in AD 934, whose ruler soon submitted. Soon after, the Scots and the Vikings who lived there rose against his rule and invaded England in AD 937. The two forces met in the famed Battle of Brunanburh, a decisive victory for the forces of Æthelstan.

This monumental victory led to the collapse of Viking power in Northern Britain. However, history is restless, and every opportunity is used. Æthelstan died in AD 939, and the Vikings promptly took control of their lost kingdom of York. We can see that in roughly 30 years, much of the Viking gains had been reversed. This example is a good insight into the nature of the Vikings' way of warfare and conquest. They relied on brute force and impulsive decisions, sweeping over England as long as their Great Heathen Army was intact. As their numbers gradually decreased, so did their victories, and many gains were lost in just a few decades.

In AD 947, however, a new wave of Vikings arrived in England. From this point on, a new chieftain appears as the great Viking leader, Eric Bloodaxe. This same year, the Northumbrians deposed King Eadred of Wessex as their ruler, making the Norwegian Eric Bloodaxe (also known as Eirik Haraldsson) their new King. It is possible, but not confirmed that Eric Bloodaxe was the son of the Norwegian King Harald Fairhair. Either way, Bloodaxe's hold on Northumbria was not as strong as he'd hoped. Due to a series of clashes with the Wessex King Eadred, he was finally expelled in AD 954, when the English again captured York. Bloodaxe was thus the last Norse King of Northumbria.

By the time Wessex's King Edgar the Peaceful came to the throne, Anglo-Saxon England saw a different political unification, which was particularly important in fighting the Viking invaders. Edgar was recognized as the King of all of England by the Anglo-Saxons and the Vikings that still dwelt in the land. However, as is often the case, this political unification and the strength of the English monarch were not always constant. Thus, after Edgar's death, the crown's strength waned, and in AD 980, the Vikings again invaded England. They likely arrived from their bases in the Isle of Man, Ireland, and Scandinavia, exploiting the English leaders' weaknesses. It was one of the first invasions after a pause of nearly 25 years. The Isle of Thanet and Hampshire are the first areas to be plundered and devastated. The conquest of England was renewed. One of the primary reasons for this new English weakness was the mysterious murder of Edgar the Peaceful's son and heir, Edward the Martyr. He was murdered at Corfe Castle in March of AD 978, which left only his inexperienced brother, Æthelred the Unready, to rule England. With this, the strong line of successors of Alfred the Great at last died out, leaving the Anglo-Saxon realm once again vulnerable to attacks. With the Norsemen looming from the foam of the sea, the kingdom's fate was again in question.

From AD 980 and on, coastal raids became frequent, first from Ireland and the isles and then from Scandinavia. Even in this advanced stage of the Viking Era, the past was repeating itself, and it was just as in the beginning, with small raiding bands sailing over, seeking silver and gold to plunder. Reports from the area tell us that seven Norse longboats sacked Southampton in AD 981, and three ships attacked Portland the following year. However, the pace soon picked up, and large fleets led by powerful nobles and chiefs ravaged England. The government of Æthelred the Unready could not fight these invaders and decided that the only viable solution was to pay them protection money, like in the past. In AD 991, they paid the Vikings £10,000, a hefty sum for the time. Almost unsurprisingly, this sum did not satisfy the cravings of the Norse. They resumed their raids and were paid, again and again, even more enormous sums than before. This led to great upheavals in English society, especially amongst the nobility, who could not keep up with the demands for more money. They voiced their anger by demanding a fight against the Vikings. To meet these demands, Æthelred the Unready declared a controversial move: to execute all Danes living in England.

The proclamation was made on St. Brice's Day in AD 1002, and the ensuing tragedy would be known as the St. Brice's Day Massacre. It was an event never before seen in Anglo-Saxon history and described as a "most just extermination of Danes who had sprung up on this island." Across the land, Danes were murdered by the dozens, many of them farmers and settlers, living there perhaps for two to three generations. Either way, scholars agree that the loss of life was significant on this day, and Danes were decimated across England. Unsurprisingly, Æthelred's controversial act had an opposite effect than what he had hoped. It provoked the hostility of the Danes across the sea. Soon after the massacre, the news reached the Danish King Sweyn Forkbeard. It is said that the Danish king's sister was living in England at the time and was a victim of the massacre. Either way, his wrath was immense, and he ordered an invasion of England in revenge. However, revenge was not his only motive. Scholars agree that the prospect of wealth and revenue was also a factor. This is further confirmed by the fact that just before the invasion, Sweyn agreed with Duke Richard II of Normandy to sell his spoils of war there untroubled.

Renewed Viking invasions began in AD 1002 and 1003. Exeter was burned down, and Hampshire, Wilton, Salisbury, and Wiltshire were devastated. In AD 1004, Sweyn's revenge army plundered East Anglia, looted Thetford and Norwich, and only then returned to

Denmark for some respite. From that year on, the Danes returned sporadically: in AD 1006-1007 and AD 1009-1012, when one Thorkell the Tall led a new Viking invasion into England. Sweyn Forkbeard also returned in AD 1013 at the head of another massive army. Seeing it, Æthelred had to leave England, fleeing to Normandy. Thus, Sweyn Forkbeard took up the vacant English throne for himself. The medieval Peterborough Chronicle writes:

"...before the month of August came king Sweyn with his fleet to Sandwich. He went very quickly about East Anglia into the Humber's mouth, and so upward along the Trent till he came to Gainsborough. Earl Uchtred and all Northumbria quickly bowed to him, as did all the people of the Kingdom of Lindsey, then the people of the Five Boroughs. He was given hostages from each shire. When he understood that all the people had submitted to him, he bade that his force should be provisioned and horsed; he went south with the main part of the invasion force, while some of the invasion force, as well as the hostages, were with his son Cnut.

After he came over Watling Street, they went to Oxford, and the town-dwellers soon bowed to him, and gave hostages. From there they went to Winchester, and the people did the same, then eastward to London."

Sweyn Forkbeard became the King of England on Christmas Day, AD 1013. He began organizing his new realm at once, but his intentions were cut short. Sweyn Forkbeard died on February 3rd, AD 1014, having reigned for only five weeks. However, his death did not loosen the Danish grip on England's throne. Even though Æthelred returned to reclaim his throne, he had to face Sweyn's son, Cnut, whom the Vikings proclaimed the new English King. Cnut and Æthelred met in the Battle of Assandun in AD 1016. It was a decisive Viking victory and cemented Cnut as the King of England. Cnut and his sons, Harthacnut and Harold Harefoot, continued to reign over the Anglo-Saxons for 26 years, from AD 1016 to 1042.

By this time, the Viking Era was entering its final stages, and a new fate awaited England, the British Isles, and Europe in general. A new threat arose, equally vicious as the Norsemen and well ahead of its time. This threat came from Normandy, across the English Channel, in the form of William the Conqueror, the young and energetic Duke of Normandy. He stood at the head of the Normans, an ethnic and cultural group from France that claimed its descent from the Vikings that settled there early in the Viking Era. They evolved into the epitome of the medieval feudal and warlike culture, with warriors that were unsurpassed in Europe. In AD 1066, following the death of the English King Edward the Confessor, William the Conqueror descended on the Anglo-Saxons and overwhelmed them in the Battle of Hastings. In turn, it was the end of many things and the beginning of others. The Anglo-Saxon kingdoms were no more, as was their identity. There were the Anglo-Normans now and the emergence of England as we know it today. It meant the end of the Viking presence in England, also. There was one last attempt at invading England again, and it also happened in AD 1066, almost a moment before the fated Norman invasion. In AD 1066, the Norwegian King Harald Hardrada sailed over the frigid North Sea in an attempt to seize the English throne in the chaos that followed the death of King Edward the Confessor. Alas, the fates were not on the side of the Vikings. Harald Hardrada was decisively beaten in the vicious Battle of Stamford Bridge, fought on September 25th, AD 1066. In this ferocious clash, Hardrada was killed, as were most of his men. It was a significant loss of life and one of the last Anglo-Saxon victories. Historians agree that Stamford Bridge is the symbol of the end of the Viking Age. It ended as it began - in bloodshed.

This is not the end of our account on the Vikings, however. This was only the account of the Vikings in England and their impact on that nation. What other countries and parts of the globe did the Vikings sail to? England was a tiny wedge of their sphere of influence and a small part of their overall story. We continue in their footsteps and follow the trails of their longships. Before we move on to further adventures, there remains a word or two concerning the Viking presence in England. We wrote about wars, invasions and endless conflict. For roughly 273 years, the Norsemen ravaged the lands of the Anglo-Saxons, but it was not all about war. There was also a great degree of cultural exchange, inter-mixing and inter-marrying.

The arrival of the Norsemen into England was a fusion of two unique cultures, a clash of worldviews and religions, which gave rise to a whole new aspect of the emerging character of England. The Vikings sought riches, gold, silver, and slaves upon their arrival. They also sought new lands to settle, farm, and raise their families so they could prosper. Many Norsemen achieved this goal and settled in some early medieval English regions. They raised homes and families, plowed the land and reaped the harvests. And many retained their old Viking customs and traditions, as well as their religion. However, many of these settlers mingled with the Anglo-Saxons they encountered in the new lands. There were marriages, and there was the emergence of a new identity. With that, it can be safely said that the modern inhabitants of England certainly have a bit of Viking blood in them, even in small amounts.

Language is one of the first aspects of a nation to be influenced by new arrivals. The impact that the Old Norse had on early English is immense. Today, we can study that impact in great detail, thanks to several factors: the many place names in England that are of Norse origins, personal names and surnames in England that are of Norse origins, and over a thousand Old Norse words that remain firmly embedded in the English vocabulary. Did you know that some of the most common English words we use today are from the Vikings? Some examples include words like fellow, beck, landing, take, steersman, busting, score, muck, aloft, skull, knife, thrust, Thursday, wrong, scathe, husband, bug, steak, choose, crawl, and many others. Also common are words such as again, awkward, fog, freckles, ransack, scowl, sister, window, gasp, and so on. As you can see, the impact of the Old Norse language is significant and used in many common English words today, and we are not even aware of their Viking origins.

Of course, placenames and toponyms of Viking origins are numerous in England and primarily found in Lincolnshire and Yorkshire, which were once within the boundaries of the so-called "Danelaw." Over 1,500 such place names are recorded, and they usually end with "-by," "-thorpe," "-thwaite," "-sty," "-fell," or "-toft." For example, Whitby, Scunthorpe, Grimsby, Cosby, Croxton, Barkby, Laxfirth, and Longhope, to name a few. Of course, in the Shetland and Orkney Islands, as well as the Hebrides, Viking place names are far more numerous and constitute almost 70-80% of all place names and toponyms. Surnames are also evidence of the Viking presence in the former parts of Danelaw.

Some earliest medieval records show that up to 60% of personal names in Yorkshire and Lincolnshire were of Scandinavian origins. Some Viking-origin surnames are Knott, Algar, Drabble, Tovey, Tubb, Rogers, Rolf, Gunn, Storey, Osmund, and many others. Many Norse surnames also end in "-sen" or "-son," meaning "son of," for example, Iverson, Hansen and Leifsson. After all, more than two centuries of inhabitance and influence will leave a lasting mark on any society. Interestingly, it should be noted that the effect the Vikings had on Anglo-Saxon culture was not entirely negative. What is more, some historians praise the positive impact that the Norse settlers had on Britain. But how?

The unique fact here is that, over time, some societies need outside influence to progress in certain areas. Whether this external influence is peaceful or violent is a different thing. In the case of the Viking invasion of Britain, the impact was both violent and peaceful. The Scandinavian settlers in their area of Danelaw were responsible for the intensification of agriculture in these areas, making Norfolk, Suffolk, and Lincolnshire some of the most prosperous regions of England at that time. Also noted is the political success of King Cnut, who regulated commerce in the North Sea waterways. After all, the impact of the Vikings on England's customs, traditions, culture, language, and politics was undeniable and remained strong throughout the Middle Ages. Then, also, there are the Normans, who originated from the Vikings in France and laid waste to Anglo-Saxon England in AD 1066, completely changing the fate of England and laying down the foundations for the nation as we know it today. We see the Vikings did, after all, shape England in a cardinal way, and with it, perhaps, the rest of the world.

As we finish the tale of Vikings in England, we must mention a critical part of the story: the famous Danegeld. This term translates roughly to "Dane Tax" or "Dane yield" and refers to the money paid to the Viking raiders so that they would leave England. This tax was collected to pay off Danish attackers and was protection money or bribery. Anglo-Saxon leaders, particularly Æthelred the Unready, quickly avoided conflict instead of paying the attackers off. By offering them a substantial quantity of silver, Æthelred thought he'd rid himself of the raiders. The effect was the opposite. The Danes thought it a fabulous arrangement. They were quick to break their promises of peace and return to the English shores with new longboats, ready to pillage. Each time they requested more significant quantities of silver so they would leave. In time, the Danegeld became an official tax, and the practice was done in Anglo-Saxon England and Francia.

Just how enormous were the amounts of silver given to the Vikings? Here are some official numbers to provide you with insight. In AD 991, Æthelred the Unready lost the Battle of Maldon to the Vikings. Seeing that he stood little chance, he was advised by the Archbishop of Canterbury to pay off the attackers rather than continue the struggle. He paid the Vikings by giving them an incredible 3,300 kilograms (7275 lbs) of silver. The Danes returned just three years later, in AD 994, besieging London. Once again, they were paid off in silver. With that, they quickly realized that extortion money was far more advantageous than simple plundering across the land, so they kept returning. In AD 1007, Æthelred gave them an incredible 13,400 kg (29,541 lbs) of silver, which gained him a mere two years of peace. These numbers only got higher as time went on. In AD 1012, they returned and were given 17,900 kg (39,462 lbs) of silver after murdering the Archbishop of Canterbury and sacking the village of Canterbury itself. Even the Norse leaders had to pay Danegeld, oddly enough. When he became King of England in AD 1016, King Cnut had to pay an enormous Danegeld of 26,900 kg (59,304 lbs) of silver under the excuse of paying his army. Simply put, it was extortion money, blackmail, bribery, or whatever you want to call it. It was the simple "law of the stronger" pay us money, or we ravage your lands. The Vikings had the power to enforce this law wherever and whenever. In time, the Danegeld stopped, as did the Vikings, but their effects were long-lasting. In summary, we will recall the famous lines of the British poet Rudyard Kipling, who tells us that "once you have paid him the Danegeld, You never get rid of the Dane." In his poem "Dane-geld," he wrote thus:

> *"We never pay any-one Dane-geld,*
> *No matter how trifling the cost;*
> *For the end of that game is oppression and shame,*
> *And the nation that plays it is lost!"*

Chapter III - The Vikings in the East

The connections between the Slavs and the Vikings run deep. They are old, reaching far back in time, standing as a testament to the differences between parallel-developing European cultures. Alas, the Norsemen's relationship with Slavic tribes was not always exemplary and, in many ways, was one-sided. The Slavs occupy a significant part of the Viking story. If it weren't for the Slavs, the Vikings would likely not achieve even half of their grand accomplishments.

The Slavs, from their earliest formation, inhabited large swaths of Europe. Better yet, they were the most numerous ethnolinguistic culture within the European continent, vastly outnumbering any other neighboring culture. Their tribes, all connected but with their differences, lived as far east as the rivers Don and Volga, their neighboring Finnic tribes and Volga Bulgars; they lived to the north, reaching Karelia and the great Lake Ladoga; far to the west, living near the Jutland Peninsula and bordering Saxons and the Danes, and thriving alongside the Elbe River; far to the South, reaching the shores of the Adriatic Sea and populating the Balkans, bordering the Byzantines and the Venetians; and all the lands in between were Slavic also - Central Europe was their core, from the shores of the frigid Baltic Sea, down to the temperate Adriatic. The Slavs originated from one unified cultural group, sharing a singular language. However, the Slavs migrated over the centuries, often adopting a semi-nomadic lifestyle, and their dialects soon grew into separate languages.

Even though their tribes numbered in the hundreds, they all shared a sense of cultural unity and bond. There needed to be more unity on the whole. This is the one thing Slavs lacked and was the primary source of their great hardships in history. Without unity, there was significant vulnerability. Another vulnerability that these tribes possessed was their lifestyle. These were no fierce warriors like the Vikings. The Slavs adopted a pastoral lifestyle in intricately connected communities, preferring to live in swampy wetlands and close to rivers. They were woodland, steppe, and waterland peoples, exceptionally skilled in sailing the rivers they lived beside, raising cattle and farming the land. These were no seafarers, no conquerors, nor invaders. All these vulnerabilities left them open to outside influence and manipulation. That was something the Vikings were exceptionally good at.

In the West, they were preyed upon by the Franks, in the south by the Byzantines, and in the North and East by Khazars and Bulgars. Now, the Vikings came as well. Almost concurrently with the early Viking arrivals into England, their longboat fleets also sailed to the east. For the most part, these were Swedish Vikings, setting sail eastwards and entering the lands of the Finns and Slavs through the Gulf of Finland. In these lands, the Norsemen could best utilize their skills as sailors: the Slavic lands were crisscrossed with rivers, lakes, and various waterways. For the Vikings, this was as good as it could get. Because waterways meant exploration, and exploration meant to raid and plunder, and raid and plunder meant prosperity. From the northern Lake Ladoga, they would sail down Volkhov and Svir, through Volga and Don, and to the mighty Dnieper. These rivers and the vast Slavic lands were the gateways to faraway realms: to the Greeks (Byzantines), the Arabs and the Bulgars, amongst others. In many ways, the land of the Slavs was the Vikings' grand entranceway to the world stage. Their entrance was always brutal and bloody, heralded by horns of war.

In the late 700s and early 800s, the Vikings entered the world stage and concurrently increased their presence in the eastern lands. At first, scholars tell us, the Slavic tribes fought the raiders off, casting them out of their lands and proving to be a tough nut to crack. The Slavs lacked unity and often warred between themselves, much to their disadvantage. The semi-legendary accounts state that they called the Vikings back, asking them to rule over them, as they could not. This, of course, is a simplified portrayal of what might have happened.

The Norsemen immersed themselves into the socio-political situation of the Slavic tribes they encountered around Lake Ladoga and beyond. Thanks to their shrewd policies, they emerged as the ruling class among them. Undoubtedly, the Norse chieftains used the chaotic situation of the Slavs to their advantage, making their lands orderly and prospering from them. That chieftain, the medieval chronicles say, was one Rurik (the Slavic rendition of the Old Norse name Hrœrekr). Medieval chronicles say that the Slavs told the Vikings thus: "Our country is rich and immense, but it is rent by disorder. Come and govern us and reign over us." So the Norse chieftain Rurik established a ruling dynasty of Rurikids that would persevere through many centuries. Some historians have proposed that this Rurik was Rorik of Dorestad, one of the competing rulers of the Norse town of Hedeby. Others, in turn, offer a theory that Rurik is not a personal name but a designation. It refers to the city of Reric, a Slav-Viking trading post that flourished in the late 700s. Thus, Rurikids could mean "Reric-men." The Norse were now the rulers of the Slavs and any other tribes in their region and sphere of influence. It is important to note here that the Slavic lands were vibrant. They had plenty of wood, ore, fish, game, exquisite furs, precious amber, and many other things sought after in international markets. That is what invited the Vikings, after all.

One thing was more precious to the Norse than anything - slaves. The Vikings were notorious slave traders, capturing "thralls," or slaves, across Europe, from Ireland to the far east. The most common slave stock of the early middle ages in Europe came from the Slavic peoples. They call themselves "Slavs" or "Sklave," the Greek rendition of their name. In the Slavic language, it means "glory," "celebration," or "people speaking the same tongue." Over the centuries, it gained a grim meaning and is now the origin of the word "slave." Slavs were captured by the hundreds and thousands, partly due to their being numerous and their lifestyle, which was not particularly warlike. Thus, the Norse ravaged their lands and took away women, children, and able-bodied men, selling them in slave markets. Such was the sad fate of these people. Now the warriors from the north who devastated them in the first place came to rule over them too.

The lands of the east had many different names. For the Vikings, it was called Austr (the East), or more commonly Garðaríki ("the realm of cities"). This last name stems from the Slavic word "gord," meaning town or fortified settlement. Their lands were thus, quite literally, the realm of towns, just as the Viking name suggests. These Norsemen were known as the Varyags, or Varangians to the Slavs. The Norse appear in early medieval chronicles under the Byzantine Greek Βάραγγος (Varangos) and Old East Slavic варягъ (varjagu). Both these terms are ultimately derived from the Old Norse term væringi, a compound of the words "var" (faith, pledge) and "gengi" (companion). This, in turn, denotes a "sworn companion," meaning "a foreigner who has taken service with a new lord."

These Varangians, these Vikings, began colonizing the eastern lands of the Slavs. They settled in Aldeigja, or Aldeigjuborg (Lake Ladoga), around AD 750 and quickly began playing an essential role in the socio-politics of the Slavic tribes. Aldeigja promptly became the principal trading port in the East and controlled the merchant routes of the entire region. Undoubtedly, it took decades for the Vikings to come out on top of the Slavic tribes. Much like in Danelaw in England, they settled the region and soon exacted tribute (i.e., protection money) from the regional tribes. The Slavs and the Finns usually paid in material goods, like furs, pelts, and amber, rather than silver or gold since they had none. A medieval chronicle reports that tribute was exacted around AD 859 and possibly earlier. As a comparison, the Danes in England exacted their Danegeld around AD 865, some 70 years after they began their vicious raids.

Around this time, the Vikings begin spreading like wildfire across Europe, making a name for themselves at the sword's tip. Of course, in time, the colonizers, being in the minority, slowly assimilated into the Slavic culture and society. A unique ruling caste emerged, Norse in origins but Slavic in its appearance and culture. It was a curious mix of Nordic and Slavic and would gradually emerge as a distinct ethnolinguistic cultural group - the Rus'. This was the Slavicized ruling elite that originated from the Viking chieftain Rurik. As you guessed, the name today is found in the names of the modern nations of Russia and Belarus. Even today, scholars are decoding the origins of the term "Rus." Is it Viking? Slavic? Something else? Some say that Rus' is a word of Finnic origin or from "Ruotsi," meaning Sweden. That word itself could stem from Old East Norse "rōþer" (Old West Norse "róðr"), which refers to rowing or a fleet levy. It could also arise from Rōþin, the name of a Swedish coastal region of Roslagen. However, (according to the author of this book) the name could be much more straightforward in origin, coming from the Slavic languages. The name Rus' could come from the Proto-Slavic word *rusъ, from the earlier form *rudsъ, both of which mean "fair-haired or blonde." The Swedish Vikings were primarily blonde or fair-haired and the first to stick with the Slavs, who gave them the simplest of names. An account by the Muslim explorer Ibn Fadlan, who encountered these Rus', indicates their appearance and could be proof that their name comes from the color of their hair and beards.

"I have seen the Rus' as they came on their merchant journeys and encamped by the Itil. I have never seen more perfect physical specimens, tall as date palms, <u>blond and ruddy</u>; they wear neither tunics nor kaftans, but the men wear a garment covering one side of the body and freeing a hand. Each man has an axe, a sword, and a knife, and keeps each by him at all times."

Either way, the Vikings were there to stay. Old Norse sagas tell us that they quickly established several important cities, almost exclusively ports, which would later become the cornerstones of the Rus' state. These were called Hólmgarðr (Slavic "Novgorod"), Holmsgardr ("Veliky Novgorod"), Kønugarðr (Kyiv), Pallteskja (Polotsk),

Aldeigjuborg (Ladoga), Smaleskja (Smolensk), Ráðstofa (Rostov), and many others. As you can see, most of these names are Norse renditions of pre-existing Slavic names, such as Smolensk and Rostov. Most of these cities have the ending - garðr, which comes from the Slavic word "gorod," i.e., fort, city, settlement.

The Vikings did not just raid, rule, and exact tribute in their new home. They lived alongside the Slavs as well and exchanged cultural traits and customs. They borrowed many words from the Old East Slavic language, many of which quickly became adopted across the Viking world. Some of these words were "torg" (marketplace, from Slavic "turgu"), "taparøx" (small axe, from Slavic "topor"), or "grikkr" (Greek). Words were not the only thing they picked up. Besides various cultural trends related to fashion and wear, they were also able to refine their seafaring skills. From the Slavs, they could learn a lot more about shipbuilding. Eventually, they adopted the style of the "lodja," a wide-bellied and shallow ship design perfected for carrying loads and trading. It was a big "game changer" for the Norse and helped expand their trade empire.

From their starting base at Aldeigja, the Rus' had many options for travel and trade. They excelled as explorers and traveled up the River Volkhov towards Holmgardr (Novgorod), and from there to Lake Ilmen and then through the River Lovat. Then they had to take a shortcut over a portage, an overland route across which they rolled their longboats on wooden logs until they reached the source of the mighty Volga River. They sailed through the territories inhabited by Permian, Slavic, and Finnic tribes, their great ships laden with trade goods such as furs, pelts, honey, and slaves. They traded with the Volga Bulgars, and then through the Volga, they reached Atil, a busy Khazar port on the shores of the Caspian Sea. From Atil, the options only increased. The Norse-Slavic Rus' joined overland caravans from there, traveling to Baghdad, where they could trade with the vast Islamic world. In many ways, the Volga River was the focal point of the rich trading world shared by the Rus', the Bulgars, and the Khazars. It was a world of opportunities from which the Vikings gained a lot, even though they were now called a different name. Through their contact with the Islamic world, the Vikings gained much wealth. Persian and Arab coins have been found across the Norse world, from England to Scandinavia. More importantly, the contact with the Islamic world left some significant descriptions of the unique Rus' culture that mixed Viking and Slavic customs into one unique ethnicity. The Persian geographer and explorer of great fame, Ibn Rustah, traveled through the Rus' lands and described their communities living along the Volga River:

"They sail their ships to ravage as-Saqaliba [the surrounding Slavs], and bring back captives whom they sell at Khazaran and Bolghar... They have no estates, villages, or fields; their only business is to trade in sable, squirrel, and other furs, and the money they take in these transactions they stow in their belts. Their clothes are clean, and the men decorate themselves with gold armlets. They treat their slaves well, and they wear exquisite clothes since they pursue trade with great energy."

We learned that the Rus' were not great farmers. Instead, their Viking roots instilled in them a need for trade and exploration, for extortion and slave trade, done at the expense of the Slavic peoples. Another account was left by Ahmad ibn Fadlan, an Arab Muslim traveler. He writes:

"On anchoring their vessels, each man goes ashore carrying bread, meat, onions, milk, and nabid [possibly, beer], and these he takes to a large wooden stake with a face like that of a human being, surrounded by smaller figures, and behind them tall poles in the ground. Each man prostrates himself before the large post and recites: 'O Lord, I have come from distant parts with so many girls, so many sable furs (and whatever other commodities he is carrying). I now bring you this offering.' He then presents his gift and continues, 'Please send me a merchant who has many dinars and dirhams, and who will trade favorably with me without too

much bartering.' Then he retires. If, after this, business does not pick up quickly and go well, he returns to the statue to present further gifts. If results continue slowly, he then presents gifts to the minor figures and begs their intercession, saying, 'These are our Lord's wives, daughters, and sons.' Then he pleads before each figure in turn, begging them to intercede for him and humbling himself before them. Often trade picks up, and he says, 'My Lord has required my needs, and now it is my duty to repay him.' Whereupon he sacrifices goats or cattle, some of which he distributes as alms. The rest he lays before the statues, large and small, and the heads of the beasts he plants upon the poles. After dark, of course, the dogs come and devour the lot -and the successful trader says, "My Lord is pleased with me, and has eaten my offerings."

This is an essential insight into Rus' customs and religious beliefs. Scholars agree that this indicates that the Rus' retained their Viking customs, centered on weapons, punishments, ship burials, and religious sacrifices. We can be thankful to the learned men of the medieval Muslim period, their travelers and explorers who ventured to faraway lands and left detailed written accounts of them. The land of the Rus', with their Viking origins, was of particular interest to them because the cultural differences with the Muslim world were immense. Ibn Khordadbeh, the famed explorer, wrote of them as well:

"They (the Rus') transport beaver hides, the pelts of the black fox and swords from the farthest reaches of the Saqaliba to the Sea of Rum [i.e., the Black Sea]. The ruler of Rum [i.e., the Byzantine Empire] takes a tithe of them. If they wish, they go to the Tnys river [i.e., "Tanais," the Greek name of the Don River], Yitil [i.e., Itil, the ancient name of the Volga], or Tin [variously identified as Don or Seversky Donets], the River of the Saqaliba. They travel to Khamlij, the city of the Khazars whose ruler takes a tithe of them. Then they betake themselves to the Sea of Jurjan [Caspian Sea], and they alight on whichever of its shores they wish. ... Sometimes, they carry their goods from Jurjan by camel to

Baghdad. Saqlab (Slavic) slaves translate for them. They claim that they are Christians and pay the jizya."

Thanks to the early Viking explorations, the eastern Rus' realms became the focal point of the great Norse trading empire. It was much-needed proof that the Vikings were not simply raiders but shrewd seafaring merchants with a penchant for exploration. Of course, much of their trade was based on human misfortune - they were predominantly slavers profiting from the servitude of others. Nevertheless, the Rus' - those descendants of the Vikings - began forming their own state. These were the earliest foundations of Kievan Rus' - the medieval predecessor of the modern nations of Belarus, Russia, and Ukraine. In its heyday, this state stretched out from Belo Ozero and Nizhny Novgorod in the East to Kiev and Pereyaslav in the South, Galich in the West, and Ladoga in the North. When Kievan Rus' was formed, the ruling Vikings were fully immersed in the Slavic culture. The ruling elite kept using Old Norse form names, but this practice was eventually dropped with the rise of Svyatoslav the Brave around the AD 950s. In simplest terms, Kievan Rus' was a multiethnic state, its inhabitants united by their recognition of the Norse Rurikid dynasty as their rulers. However, after just a few generations, much of the original Viking identity was lost in the Rurikids, and they gradually became fully Slavic. As the noted historian F. Donald Logan summarizes: "in AD 839, the Rus' were Swedes (Vikings); in AD 1043, the Rus' were Slavs."

After the Viking chieftain Rurik, the initial ruler over the Slavs, came his son Igor (Old Norse Ingvar) and his regent Oleg (Helgi). After them came the great Svyatoslav, the first Rurikid ruler with a Slavic name, whose sons fought bitterly for the throne. With the rise of Vladimir the Great, Svyatoslav's victorious son, the Kievan Rus' officially became a Christian nation following the ruler's baptism. The Kievan Rus' persevered until it was destroyed by a Mongol Invasion in AD 1240. As we can see, this endeavor of the Vikings proved much more successful and different than the events that unfolded in England around the same time. However, we leave the story of the Kievan Rus' for another time. It is not a story of the Vikings but of the Slavs, where Norse origins quickly became a distant memory. We can only wonder what the world would look like if the Vikings did not settle amongst the Slavs. How would history have unfolded then?

Chapter IV: The Vikings in the Faroe Islands and Iceland

From their homes in Norway, Denmark, and Sweden, the Vikings always looked beyond the turbulent waves of the seas and oceans, wondering what faraway realms lay beyond. We can only imagine how little boys and grown men fantasized about some rich and wondrous lands beyond the great east oceans. With the onset of the Viking Age, they could finally set sail into the unknown, braving the waves and tempting fate as they searched for these distant realms. What they discovered, however, was far from glorious, but it was good enough for a home. The Faroe Islands lay roughly halfway between Iceland and Norway and were thus on an almost direct path on the journeys of the Vikings. They are also close to the Shetlands and the Orkneys, and thus to Scotland, which was also a crucial part of Norse history. We can understand that the Faroe Islands were destined to be discovered. By the time the Norse spotted them, they were, for the most part, uninhabited. What could be seen from the longships was promising. It was an archipelago with islands big and small, fertile and green, and rich with sheep, fish, and nesting birds. Were they devoid of man? Some scholars and historians suggest that the Norse were not the first men to set foot on the Faroe Islands. Specific evidence suggests that Irish hermits and monks dwelt on the island several centuries before the Vikings appeared. Archeological excavations yielded interesting results in the form of petrified barley and peat ash, as well as sheep bones and DNA. These dated to roughly AD 500, long before the Vikings ventured from their homes in the mid-700s. These finds could be a missing link to confirm that ascetic monks from Ireland and Scotland, seeking solitude and isolation, sailed in their ramshackle coracles towards the remote Faroe Islands, living there in complete separation from the rest of the world. In truth, they must have introduced the sheep to the islands, whoever lived there in a semi-feral state. A vague idea of faraway islands lying to Scotland's north has been present in the British Isles well before the Vikings, but nothing definite was written down. The first written mention of what is undoubtedly the Faroe Islands is dated to AD 825, when an Irish monk Dicuil, in his work Liber de Mensura Orbis Terrae (Description of the Sphere of the Earth), writes the following account:

"Many other islands lie in the northerly British Ocean. One reaches them from the northerly islands of Britain, by sailing directly for two days and two nights with a full sail in a favorable wind the whole time... Most of these islands are small, they are separated by narrow channels, and for nearly a hundred years hermits lived there, coming from our land, Ireland, by boat. But just as these islands have been uninhabited from the beginning of the world, so now the Norwegian pirates have driven away the monks; but countless sheep and many different species of sea-fowl are to be found there..."

The exact date of the Viking settlement of the Faroe Islands is not known with certainty but can be safely assumed to be around AD 825 or earlier. This was a time when the Vikings spread across Europe in every direction, somewhere raining death, elsewhere settling peacefully. In the case of the Faroe Islands, it was definitely the latter version. The Norse origins of the Faroe Islands are mentioned in the famed Norse Sagas, chiefly in the "Færeyinga saga" (now lost), as well as in the "Flateyjarbók" and the "Saga of Óláfr Tryggvason." All of these sources state that the Viking to first settle in the islands was one Grímur (Grimr) Kamban. While his name is undoubtedly Norse, his surname is Gaelic and comes from the word "cambán," meaning "crooked one." Whether this Grimr was a Viking from Ireland or the Isle of Man or gained this nickname from the Irish monks already living on the isle, we do not know. We also don't know whether the Vikings came as raiders, explorers, or settlers. If Irish monks lived there at the time, it is doubtful that they had any particular riches to be plundered, as they were likely anchorites. However, it is agreed that the monks soon abandoned the Faroe Islands entirely due to the increased presence of the Norsemen. This could have been fueled by fears of a fate similar to the raided monasteries in Lindisfarne and Iona decades before.

Either way, the Faroe Islands soon became a known location on the Viking voyages, and settlers began arriving sporadically. Also, the islands could have gained their name at this very time, just as they are called today. Faroe could come from the Norse words "far," meaning livestock, and "oy," meaning islands. What is interesting is that settlers from all across the Norse world came here for varied reasons. Settlers came from Viking settlements in Ireland, the Isles, and the Isle of Man. These were the so-called "Norse-Gaels," a mix between the Vikings and the native Gaelic speakers. Settlers also came from Norway and elsewhere. The settlement could have intensified in the ninth century when people from Norway sought to flee from the oppressive rule of King Harald Fairhair. By then, they already knew of the Faroe Islands as a possible location, which they chose as their new home.

We know this from historical accounts. Even though the Faroe Islands were fertile, the people living there still had to import certain goods. Barley, for example, was imported from Norway, meaning a trade network was extant throughout the period. The Norse settlers were skilled farmers and pastoralists. An abundance of crops was farmed on the Faroe Island's rich soils. Also, many cows, pigs, goats, and sheep were raised. Of course, the settlers had to adapt to their surroundings. What few trees that did exist on the islands were soon used up, which meant that peat and other resources had to be used for heating. Alternate food sources, such as puffins and an abundance of fish, were also discovered. Indeed, the Norse settlers made do and lacked but little.

Interestingly, the Viking settlers of the Faroe Islands were not involved in any major conflicts, raids, or wars, contrary to most other Norse "endeavors." Pretty much left to their interests, the Faroe settlers developed independently, often influenced by the events unfolding in Norway. It was a great "experiment," showing us how a Viking nation could develop when focused on everyday life and not raiding and constant exploitation. There were, of course, some sporadic internal conflicts in the islands, and the Faroe's history does boast some true Viking heroes. One of the foremost of these is the famed Tróndur í Gøtu, a folk hero and the main protagonist of the Færeyinga saga. A Viking chieftain born in AD 945, he was a staunch heathen and preserver of Nordic traditions. However, he soon came into conflict with a rival Faroese chieftain, Sigmundur Brestisson, the man who was the key proponent of the Christianization of the islands. The saga is centered on their struggle and the stubborn defiance of Tróndur í Gøtu, who opposed the new religion to the last. This proud warrior single-handedly staved off the arrival of the Christian faith to the Pagan islands but, in the end, could not succeed. Even today, there is a saying in the Faroese and Icelandic languages: vera einhverjum Þrándur í Götu ("being someone's Þrándur í Götu:) or just - að vera þrándur í götu ("to be a þrándur í götu"), means to be an obstacle to somebody. After all, isn't that the true Viking spirit?

Although a successful settlement, the Faroe Islands were in no way a serious challenge. The islands proved to be a convenient way station on the crossroads of the Viking waterways, and their settlement by the Norse was more or less expected. After all, they weren't all that far from pre-existing Norse settlements. There was an island, further to the northwest, more remarkable than any discovered before, but also more challenging and more remote, just waiting for the eventual arrival of the Norse longships. That island was modern-day Iceland. Lying just 420 kilometers west of the Faroe Islands, this new island proved to be the next destination for the restless Viking explorations.

Iceland is a rugged and geologically unique island. It has a subarctic climate and is full of volcanoes, hot springs, and vast plains of inhospitable landscapes. Only its "edges" are habitable and suited for life. Most of modern Iceland's cities are situated precisely there. Despite all this, that did not stop the Vikings from calling it their new home. According to the Medieval Icelandic saga called Landnamabok, the first to discover the island was a Viking settler from the Faroe Islands, one Naddodd. He was returning from Norway back to the Faroe Islands, but drifted off-course and got lost, until he reached the shores of a land never before seen. Observing its hellish landscapes and icy plains, he named it "Snowland". He found no trace of human habitation there and decided to leave. No humans meant that the Norse could claim this land for their own, without resorting to invasion and conflict. Even though the Norse were seemingly the first to discover Iceland, archeological evidence suggests otherwise. Yet again, just as it was with monks of the Faroe Islands, the Scot-Irish hermit monks seemingly dwelt in Iceland at least a century before Naddodd discovered it by chance. Always seeking seclusion and isolation, these solitary ascetic monks left their traces in Iceland. How they found Iceland is unknown, but evidence at the remote Kverkarhellir Cave speaks of their presence. In this somber cavern, they carved distinct Celtic-style crosses, the only consolation they had in the inhospitable land. As soon as the Norse arrived, the Irish monks were gone for good, in search for a new desolate place to dwell in.

After Naddodd's chance discovery, word spread of a vast island to the west of the Faroe Islands. Restless as they were, Viking explorers quickly sought it out. The following Viking explorer to reach Iceland did so also by accident. He was called Garðar Svavarsson, a Danish man, married to a woman from the Hebrides in Scotland. Around AD 860, he set sail towards the Hebrides to claim an inheritance, but as he crossed the treacherous passage between mainland Scotland and the Orkneys, Garðar Svavarsson was thrown far off course after a violent storm caught his ship. Forced to sail on a northerly course due to the storm, he eventually reached the shores of this new land. He continued sailing alongside its shoreline, effectively circumnavigating it. This informed him know that the new land was an island. Svavarsson landed on Iceland's northern coast, where he made a temporary house and stayed throughout the winter. Today this place is called Húsavík ("House Bay"). It was the first place to be settled by Norsemen in Iceland. As spring arrived, Svavarsson returned home and spoke of a new land he found, praising it and calling it Garðarshólmi, after himself.

Even though Svavarsson's discovery was accidental, no other Viking sailed there with intent until Hrafna-Flóki Vilgerðarson. Having heard Svavarsson's tales of a vast new land far to the west, Flóki decided to take his own family, set sail on a big expedition, and settle it if possible. He was accompanied by his wife Gró, their two children Oddleifur and Þjóðgerður, and three men – Herjólfr, Faxi, and Þórólfr (Thorolf). Together, they raised the sails on their longship and ventured forth from Western Norway, setting a course for the Shetland Islands. The medieval Icelandic Landnámabók saga describes his journey and tells us that Flóki met misfortune early in his journey when, in the Shetlands, his daughter drowned. Undaunted, he continued his journey and reached the Faroe Islands. Still devoted to his mission, Flóki acquired three ravens while at the Faroe Islands, restocking his resources. As in the Biblical story of Noah, using ravens to find land was an old tactic used by the Viking explorers. When searching for landfall, a sailor would let loose a raven. If the bird took off in a particular direction and did not return, it was a sure sign that it reached land, and they would follow that due course.

It was because of his ravens that Flóki thus earned his famous nickname, Hrafna-Flóki ("Raven-Floki"). One can only imagine such an exploratory expedition's daring, adventurous spirit in the ninth century. Because of his bravery and desire to explore, Flóki earned a name worthy of praise. He was armed with the famed Viking decisiveness and the fiery spirit of boldness. We can almost envision a group of rugged, grim Norsemen as they cut through the waves of the

Atlantic in their dragon-headed longship, battered by the waves and the sprinkle of salt water. Crossing the North Atlantic's vastness was reserved only for the bravest. Just imagine the tumultuous waters, the black storms brewing on the distant horizon. A man had to possess great courage and dedication to master his fears and conquer such a vast and unruly aspect of nature. That is the perfect way to describe Viking seafarers: courageous, confident, and daring.

Hrafna-Flóki, seeing no land in any direction, alone between the water and the sky, clung to a ragged hope that land would soon be found. That, and a promise of a better life. After a while, Hrafna-Flóki decided to utilize his ravens. The first raven wheeled around and flew back towards the Faroe Islands. The second returned to the ship. Both meant that land was still not close. After a while, Floki released his third and final raven. This time, the bird did not return. It was the sign that they needed. In the end, Floki discovered the island of the tales and became the first Viking to intentionally reach Iceland, that distant northern land. He and his crew came upon a large bay opposing the modern capital of Iceland, Reykjavik.

Settling in the western area full of fjords, he, his family, and crew spent a whole summer and an entire winter in the new land. Later, he said that the summer was satisfactory and temperate, with plenty of fish, fowl, and other food to be acquired. The winter, though, was particularly harsh. When the spring finally came, Flóki and his family and crew returned to Norway to recount their deeds and proclaim their discovery. Before departing, Floki named the island "Iceland," due to the abundance of ice he spotted in the distance. This is how the Vikings discovered their northernmost home, far from Scandinavia.

The first Norseman to leave Scandinavia to settle permanently in Iceland was one Ingólfr Arnarson. It is commonly agreed that he settled in Iceland in AD 874, settling in a fjord that he named Reykjavik (Smoke Bay).

*There was a man of the North [Norway], Ingólfr, who is truly said to be
the first to leave it for Iceland, in the time when Haraldr the Fair-Haired
was sixteen winters of age [...] he settled south in Reykjavík. —*
Íslendingabók

With him came other settlers, and Iceland soon became a new
Norse colony. There were several reasons why this new land seemed
promising to settlers. Firstly, the rise of centralized rule in Norway,
especially during the time of Harald Fairhair, meant that more and
more Norse wanted to find a different home for themselves, fleeing
oppression. Secondly, the continued resistance against Viking
settlements in Anglo-Saxon England meant that the Norse wanted to
find a more peaceful solution in a land where there were no direct
enemies to face. Thirdly, Scandinavia's lack of arable land forced
families to seek new opportunities elsewhere. Fourthly, the promise of
successful trade in Iceland attracted Norse merchants. The island was
rich in fish, fowl, and sought-after goods such as walrus ivory.

Lastly, the remoteness of Iceland was attractive to Vikings who
wanted to flee from blood feuds, crimes, debts, and the like. Therefore,
Iceland was fully settled in no time. The medieval chronicles tell us that
this occurred by AD 930. It is possible that Arnarson came at the head
of a fleet of settlers, perhaps some 300 to 400 strong. Landnámabók
lists 435 men as the initial settlers, most settling in the northern and
southwestern parts of the island. Due to the vastness of the island, lands
were either claimed freely, purchased from the first settlers, or taken by
threats or force. Some settlers claimed more land than they could ever
use, so they gave it away. Scholars suggest that around 24,000 people
could have settled in Iceland in the following decades. Interestingly,
these immigrants did not come from Scandinavia exclusively. Modern
genealogical research from Iceland tells us that many settlers came from
Scotland, Ireland, the Orkneys, and surrounding areas. Of these, many
could have been Gaelic thralls, slaves in service to Viking settlers. A
solid portion of modern Icelandic DNA is thus Gaelic in origin.

Quickly, Iceland proved one of the most prosperous and flourishing of all Viking colonies. From its settlement in AD 874 until 930, when the settling was essentially complete, Iceland grew into a prosperous young "nation." In AD 930, the most powerful chieftains of Iceland created a yearly assembly called Alþingi (Althing). This was an early form of a parliament, which convened every summer at the Þingvellir. Here, elected representatives could amend laws, settle major disputes, preside over lawsuits and trials, and dispense justice. These early Norse laws were not written down but memorized by a specially appointed "Lawspeaker." The Icelandic Althing is considered the world's oldest existing parliament. From AD 930 to roughly 1262, Iceland experienced its Golden Age, called the Commonwealth Years. In this period, this Norse colony developed independently and enjoyed prosperity. Also, during this time, some of the most famous Icelandic sagas were penned down, describing the exploits of Icelandic Vikings, who went exploring faraway places. Of those, we shall write also.

The prosperous Icelandic Commonwealth Years ended, sadly, in bloodshed. Towards the end of this period began the so-called "Age of the Sturlungs," a 42 to 44-year civil war and internal strife amongst Iceland's most powerful noble families. Ever since the settlement, the farming families prospered. By the AD 1200s, just a few families held all the power, rising in fame, wealth, and prosperity. The power was in their hands. The end of the Commonwealth began with the rise of Snorri Sturluson, the famed member of the Sturlung dynasty. He became the vassal of King Haakon IV of Norway, who wanted to exert his power over Iceland. The Sturlungs attempted to enforce his rule among the Icelanders by force, leading to a civil war. During this clash, several battles were fought, notably the Battle of Örlygsstaðir, the Battle of the Gulf in AD 1244, and the Battle of Haugsnes in AD 1246. These were some of the fiercest clashes in the entire history of Iceland. In the end, the Icelanders signed the Old Covenant in AD 1264, which affected the union of Norway and Iceland. With this, the political model of Iceland shifted towards monarchy, as the local chieftains lost their power.

In general, Iceland and its rich history are the perfect examples of what the Vikings were capable of when they did not resort to simple raiding and extortion. When left to simple exploration, they were quick to discover new and faraway lands and, no matter how inhospitable they were, make a settlement and a colony that was sure to prosper. The Faroe Islands were like a test - a halfway base from which new explorations could be launched. Whichever new colony the Norse founded, it was quickly integrated into the pre-existing network of the Norse world, immersed into its unique religion, culture, and language. Last but not least, thanks to the peacefully developing Norse realm in Iceland, many Norse sagas were penned down and saved for posterity. Many extant Norse sagas were written down in the Middle Ages in Iceland, where they were preserved. Many exist, some of which are Króka-Refs saga, Hávarðar saga Ísfirðings, Egils saga Skalla-Grímssonar, Bjarnar saga Hítdælakappa, Þorsteins saga Síðu-Hallssonar, and many others. Without these sagas, we would not know as much as we do about the Vikings' explorations of North America, their settlement of Greenland, and the early events and developments of Norse Iceland. Of course, these famed sagas would not exist if it weren't for brave Norsemen who defied the odds of destiny.

Chapter V: To Faraway Realms - The Norse in Greenland

What happened when the Norse settled in Iceland? If you think they parted with their restless ways and resorted simply to farming and surviving, you'd be wrong. After all, it is difficult to subdue that restless Viking spirit that yearns for sailing, exploration, and battle. Initially, it was thought Iceland was the "land at the end of the world," so remote and inhospitable that no other habitable lands were ever likely to exist. Rumors spoke differently. The Icelanders didn't fear; they unfurled their longships' sails and ventured across the northern ocean's turbulent and icy waves. They saw a more harsh and remote land than even Iceland was - Greenland.

Situated between the Arctic and Atlantic oceans, this remote North American island is primarily covered by the only permanent ice sheet outside Antarctica. Its coastlines are habitable, with fertile ground and plenty of animals and fish that the Vikings always subsisted on. It was only a matter of time before the Icelanders would discover it in their westerly explorations. The first Viking said to have found Greenland was Gunnbjörn Ulf-Krakuson, a Norwegian who settled in Iceland. While traveling to Iceland, he was blown off course and reached a new land. He noted it but did not make landfall. The given dates for this discovery are between AD 876 and 932. Since Greenland is physically a part of the North American continent, it could be said that Ulf-Krakuson was the first man ever to discover the continent. Either way, he reported his discovery back home in Iceland, and that was that. However, another Icelander would decide to investigate this find soon after and settle if possible. Snæbjörn galti Hólmsteinsson, whose exploits were penned down into a saga, has sadly been lost to time. It is said that this Norseman sailed to Greenland intentionally in AD 978. He supposedly made a settlement there, but the attempt ended in a disaster, but what type of disaster we do not know. He could have been thwarted by the weather, harsh conditions, internal strife, or any number of other things.

This did not dissuade the other Icelanders from attempting to colonize this new land. The first permanent settler of Greenland was the famed Viking Erik the Red. His deeds are preserved in the famous "Saga of Erik the Red," called so because of the color of his beard. Erik the Red was born in Rogaland, Norway; however, his father was exiled soon after his birth for committing manslaughter. His first choice for his family's new home in exile was Iceland. Erik the Red grew up there and had a home in Haukadalr, also known as Hawksdale. Erik the Red was also a restless Norseman. He soon got into a bitter feud with a neighbor, which ended in the neighbor's bloodshed. Just like his father in years past, Erik was also banished from the land. It is this that led to his eventual settlement of Greenland.

Erik the Red set sail for the land first discovered by Hólmsteinsson due to its relative proximity to Iceland. For three years of his exile, Erik the Red explored the coastlines of this new land, spending winter in the many fjords and eventually naming the land "Greenland." He created the name deliberately, as it sounded more appealing than Iceland. He wanted to create a colony and hoped to attract potential settlers with a good reputation. His idea worked! Many Viking families in Iceland who were poor or lived on land unsuitable for farming heard about this new land and chose to accompany him to Greenland and start a new colony there. Erik gathered enough settlers for 25 ships and returned to Greenland in AD 985. Only 14 of those ships made it to the destination, where the immigrants soon founded two settlements: the Western one (to the north) and the Eastern one (to the south). The Norse were spread around the many fjords in their small villages and farmsteads. Life in Greenland was not easy, but it was still possible. The coastal areas were green and fertile, and the land was rich in walruses, seals, fish, whales, and other creatures that the Vikings could hunt for food and trade.

Life in Greenland might seem impossible, but the Norse made it happen. Against all odds, their colony in Greenland persevered for several centuries. Modern estimates suggest that the settlement in Greenland numbered between 2,000 (at the lowest) and 10,000 inhabitants in its heyday. As mentioned, these people lived in two separate regions, the Western and Eastern Settlements. There also existed a smaller, Middle Settlement. Archeological excavations in all these regions have so far identified the remains of roughly 620 separate farms. Of these, 500 were located in the more prosperous Eastern Settlement, 95 were in the Western one, and around 20 in the so-called Middle Settlement. These regions, or "settlements," were chosen by the Vikings as the most favorable areas of the coastline for habitation. They were similar to their homelands in Norway and Iceland, full of fjords and green valleys. In these fjords they spread out their farms, coexisting in peace and prosperity. They became the Norse Greenlanders, a remote part of the wider Viking world.

The Norse Greenlanders thrived for the most part, and when necessary, they could make ends meet. Their economy was dependent on both hunting and fishing, as well as farming and pastoralism. The Norse brought cattle, sheep and goats and raised them in vast numbers for milk from which cheese and butter could be made. Research also shows that most of the meat these people consumed was either from the caribou or seals they hunted regularly. Fish, of course, was a significant part of their diet. It is known that the Viking hunters made annual trips to the icy north of Greenland, where they gathered seal and whale meat and hunted walruses, narwhals, and polar bears, for their meat, hides, and the ivory of their tusks. These latter items were prized as export goods and traded across the Norse trade networks. It is fascinating how quickly the Vikings could establish a functioning colony that would excel in trade. Though remote, the Greenlanders exported sheep, seals, wool, rope, ivory, and cattle hides. Of course, many other things had to be imported in return, such as wood, iron, food, and news. The Norse also traded with the native inhabitants of Greenland, although their relationship is poorly documented and might not have always been peaceful.

The Norse colony in Greenland prospered for several centuries after its inception around AD 1000. Yet - it failed in the end. The settlements were abandoned, and their inhabitants were either dead or gone. Why? Researchers are still piecing together that puzzle, with several likely causes. Firstly - the climate. Around the end of the 14th and the beginning of the 15th centuries, the temperature in Greenland became substantially colder. This was a specific period known today as the Little Ice Age. This brought a sudden decline in Greenland's community. The smaller Western Settlement was abandoned around AD 1350, leaving only the Eastern Settlement to survive.

Almost three decades later, the people of the Eastern Settlement suffered a devastating attack from the native Inuits in AD 1379. This attack resulted in the death of 18 men and the burning of several houses and churches. Soon after, the Greenlanders began to dwindle. However, we do not know what happened to them. A likely assumption is that they emigrated to Iceland or elsewhere. The last known written record of Norse Greelnaders is dated to AD 1408 and mentions a marriage made in AD 1408 in the church at Hvalsey. The ruins of this church are the best preserved in Greenland and can still be seen today. After this mention in AD 1408, few or no written records mention the Greenlanders or their fate. Only a few extant pieces of evidence are related to Greenland in later times. It is supposed that some Norse still lived there, as a letter dated AD 1448 indicates. In this letter, the bishops of two Icelandic episcopal sees are instructed to provide the "inhabitants of Greenland" with a priest and a bishop, as they did not have them for roughly 30 years after an attack from "heathens" who destroyed most of the churches and took the populace prisoner. This could be the supposed attack by the Inuit. Still, it is commonly agreed that by the middle or end of the 15th century, the Eastern settlement in Greenland was also defunct and largely abandoned. Still, nothing is known for sure, and the fate of the Greenlanders is still somewhat veiled in mystery. Another mention is dated to the 1540s when a ship landed in what was once the Eastern Settlement and discovered the corpse of a Norseman.

Of course, over the years, many plausible causes of the demise of the Greenlanders were proposed, and they all likely played a role. They could have lacked enough support from their homeland, partly because of their remoteness. Some offered that they were also ravaged by marauding European pirates who could've taken the populace prisoner. Another unique theory suggests that the Greenlanders failed to adapt to the growing cold and rejected the Inuit way of clothing. Those that accepted it eventually intermarried with the Inuit and were assimilated. This theory is not widely accepted, as there is no logical reason for the Greenlanders to fail to adapt to the weather conditions, especially not after several centuries of living there and enduring. After all, this is nearly half a millennium that the Norse dwelt in Greenland.

Their fate remains a mystery. We know that their pastoral way of life would have been greatly affected by the "Little Ice Age" as the temperatures dropped significantly in summer and winter. This could have meant a sharp decrease in their livestock. DNA research on human remains from Greenland suggests that during the colony's later stages, the marine-based protein found predominantly in seal meat became a significant part of their diet. The earlier periods, however, show a stark contrast with the majority of land-based proteins consumed. Sea voyages could have also suffered with the "Little Ice Age" and worsening weather conditions. This could mean that the Greenlanders received fewer visiting ships from Iceland and Norway, and their travel too was limited.

Moreover, the old and adopted travel routes alongside Greenland's coasts were hampered because of the increasing quantities of ice. In the end, it seems that the governments of Iceland and Norway left the Greenlanders to fend for themselves, abandoning their cause. A letter from AD 1448 mentions Greenland as "a region situated at the uttermost end of the earth." A similar letter dated around AD 1500, written by Pope Alexander VI, again mentions Greenland. The Pope writes of his belief that no communion had been performed in Greenland for a century and that no ship had visited there for the past 80 years. Of course, there is other evidence for the colony's demise. One of the farms was covered in layers of drifting sand up to 10 feet deep. This could suggest that Norse farming and deforestation had led to soil erosion and desertification, which would be fatal for the colony's life. One striking archeological discovery is the final, sad insight into the fate of Norse Greenland. At one of the larger inland farms, archeologists discovered the remains of a solitary Norseman. He appears to have lain down, died at the entrance of his home, and was left unburied. This is a clear indication that there was no one else left to bury the poor man. Was he the last of the Norse Greenlanders? Was he a stubborn older man who would not abandon remote Greenland, the home of his forebears?

Whatever the reasons, one thing remains certain, the Norse colony of Greenland was gone. After nearly 500 years of existence, it vanished under mysterious circumstances. Here, we see that not all Vikings' endeavors were successful. Did the Norse "bite off more than they could chew"? Was Greenland simply too remote and inhospitable to be successful? We might never know, but we can still admire the persistence and the brave, adventurous spirit of the Vikings, who did not hesitate to sail to the very ends of the world - whatever may come.

Chapter VI: Beyond the Edges of the Earth - The Vikings Discover America

You must be wondering if Greenland was their final endeavor. Wondering if the Vikings realized the remoteness of this faraway island and did not venture any further. Well, if you think this, you're wrong. They did sail onward. After all, as long as there are sails, favorable winds, and the open ocean, no self-respecting Viking would shy away from the prospect of fame, riches, and new bountiful lands to settle. We begin yet another chapter of the Vikings' westerly voyages. This time, it was from their homes in Greenland that they sailed onward, discovering the land we know today as North America, and quite a while before its subsequent "discovery" by Christopher Columbus. If we observe the modern maps of the region, we can see that Greenland is somewhat "close" to the very north of North America. The island is considered a part of this continent. It should not be surprising to know that the Norse set foot in America, discovering new areas and marveling upon the land's riches.

Not too long after settling in Greenland, the Norse set sail again, going further and further every time, exploring and returning to their settlements. In no time, new discoveries appeared. One of the first Vikings to spot North America was one Bjarni Herjólfsson, a merchant from Norway. He arrived in Iceland one day to meet his father there but soon found out that his father had settled in the new colony of Greenland. Bjarni sailed to Greenland. However, he was blown off course, and after three days of sailing, he spotted a new land that he knew wasn't Greenland. He could see mountains, hills, and thick forests but did not set foot on it. Upon his return to Greenland and then Norway, word spread of a new land rich in timber. This prospect was especially interesting for the Greenlanders since they lacked wood. It was up to the Greenland Vikings to explore the western seas and discover this land. Who better to do it than the sons of the famed explorer Erik the Red? The first of them to embark on the journey was Leif Erikson, who showed great interest in Bjarni's tale. At first, it was supposed that Erik himself accompanied his son, but he chose not to. His son purchased a boat from Bjarni, hired a crew of 35 men, and ventured forth. Soon after, he discovered the same lands Bjarni did and explored them. The first he found was not promising. It was an icy land filled with rock. He named it "Helluland," meaning "Stone-Slab Land." Today, it is believed these were the barren shores of Baffin Island, which, naturally, were of no interest to the Norsemen.

"They sailed away from land; then to the Vestribygd and to Bjarneyjar [the Bear Islands]. Thence they sailed away from Bjarneyjar with northerly winds. They were out at sea for two half-days. Then they came to land, rowed along it in boats, explored it, and found there flat stones, many and so great that two men might lie on them stretched on their backs with heel to heel. Polar foxes were there in abundance. This land they gave name to and called it Helluland [stone-land]."

Leif followed the coastline and came upon a promising land he named "Markland," meaning "The Land of Forests." As the name suggests, this was a heavily forested land, which they quickly marked as great interest for the Greenlanders, who were sorely lacking wood. Today, it is believed that Markland was the Labrador Peninsula. Leif continued to sail south until he came upon land that was the most promising of all. It had everything needed to live a good life, and the Norse were delighted at the idea of a new colony.

"The nature of the country was, as they thought, so good that cattle would not require house feeding in winter, for there came no frost in winter, and little did the grass wither there. Day and night were more equal than in Greenland or Iceland."

Leif and his crew discovered grapes in this new land, the saga says. He named the land "Vinland," meaning "The Land of Wine." Today, we believe that this was the Great North Peninsula of Newfoundland island. The name's origins are disputed, and Vinland could also mean the land of pastures. Either way, Leif Erikson and his crew spent a winter in this new land, sometime around AD 1000. The location of their stay is unknown but is speculated to be somewhere near Cape Bauld, on the northern tip of Newfoundland. One day, the sagas say, Leif's foster father Tyrker was found completely drunk on something called "wine berries." This could have been a variety of berries that grow in the area, such as gooseberries, squashberries, or cranberries. These also could have been naturally fermented and thus mistaken by the Norsemen as "wine."

Leif spent the winter noting that the area was more mild and the conditions more favorable than in Greenland. In the springtime, he returned to Greenland successfully and spread the word of his discoveries. For some time, the Norsemen discussed the opportunities of the new lands. Leif Erikson's brother, Thorvald, states that further exploration of this "Vinland" must be performed. Leif offers him his ship, and Thorvald accepts and sails west with a crew of 30 men. They safely reach Vinland and spend a winter there, subsisting easily on fish and other local foods. When spring arrived, Thorvald and his men explored the land, going further and more in-depth than Leif and his men. Even though they made extensive explorations, Thorvald failed to spot any signs of other humans.

Thorvald and his men lived at their camp for another winter through the following summer, making further explorations but in a different direction. This time, however, they encountered the Native American people who lived in the area. The contact, however, was not peaceful. Thorvald's crew encounters three skin-covered canoes and three natives sleeping under each one. For unknown reasons, the Vikings attack the natives, killing eight of the men. The ninth one manages to escape them.

"Thorvald then said: "Here it is beautiful, and here would I like to raise my dwelling." Then went they to the ship and saw upon the sands within

the promontory three elevations, and went thither, and saw there three skin boats (canoes), and three men under each. Then divided they their people, and caught them all, except one, who got away with his boat. They killed the other eight, and then went back to the cape, and looked round them, and saw some heights inside of the firth, and supposed that these were dwellings."

They called these natives skrælingjar (Skraelings), a name possibly stemming from the Old Norse word skrækja, meaning "bawl, shout, or yell," and referring to the native's tradition of screaming when going to battle. Soon enough, the natives return in force, attacking the Viking group. The Native Americans launched many arrows at the Norsemen and eventually withdrew. In the attack, Thorvald Erikson is mortally wounded and eventually dies. Thorvald's men bury him in Vinland and return to Greenland after another long winter. The Vikings and the Native Americans had unbridgeable differences between them, and conflict soon erupted. This did not stop further Norse explorers from trying to claim Vinland for themselves.

Enter Thorfinn Karlsefni Thórdarson. This influential and ambitious man from Norway was very keen on being the first to settle Vinland permanently, after hearing tales of this faraway land. In true Viking fashion, he embarks on an ambitious voyage of exploration. His attempt is more serious: around AD 1010, he supplies three ships with goods and livestock; other ships take some 160 men and women on the incredible voyage from Greenland. In time, they reach Vinland in good condition and settle at the same place Leif did before them. They winter there without difficulties, and while they explore their surroundings, they also meet the natives. Their first contact is more peaceful. The natives approach them with intent to trade, carrying furs and gray squirrel skins. The Vikings offer them milk and red cloth in exchange, of which the latter was never before seen by the Indigenous people. They are fascinated by the red cloth and tie it around their heads. All seems well, but the contact soon turns sour.

The Saga of Erik the Red and the Greenlanders' Saga give conflicting accounts of what happened. One states that the natives tried the milk, but it made them ill. This, in turn, made the natives angry. The other saga says that the natives wanted to trade for the Norse weapons, but the Norse rejected the idea. There is also the tale of a bull belonging to the Vikings. The bull got loose, frightening the natives, who quickly fled the scene. Whichever saga is correct, the conflict between the two groups erupted again. The Native Americans came in great numbers and assaulted the Norse, who had difficulty defending themselves. In the end, however, the Norse prevailed, and the attack was thwarted. Thorfinn and his group stay longer in Vinland, where Thorfinn's wife gives birth to their son, Snorri. This is the first Norse to be born in North America. Eventually, the expedition heads back to the relative safety of Greenland. Thorfinn Karlsefni never returned to Vinland. The sagas say that he made a good profit from his voyage, likely bringing back substantial trade goods and that he settled with his wife and child in Iceland and lived prosperously.

Historians attempted to discover the remnants of Norse activity in North America for many years. The content of the sagas that describes these explorations has been considered credible and based on actual events, therefore, giving us no reason to doubt them. Where exactly did the Norsemen make their camps during the winter? Over the decades, many sporadic finds were made but did not indicate an actual Viking settlement. Several items of a possible Norse origin have been discovered in Canada's north, in sites belonging to Native Americans. These were the proof that some trade or contact existed between the natives and the Norse. It wasn't until the 1960s that the first considerable discovery was made at the famed L'Anse aux Meadows site. Situated on the northern tip of Newfoundland, this Norse site is the only confirmed one in North America outside Greenland.

A husband-and-wife archeology team from Norway, Helge and Anne Stine Ingstad have spent years trying to deduce the exact site of Vinland and the Norse camps. In 1960 they got lucky, as a Newfoundland native, the citizen of a tiny fishing hamlet of L'Anse aux Meadows, one George Decker, led the pair to a group of mounds close to the village. The people there called it simply the "old Indian camp." The mounds were covered in grass but were a distinctive sign of an ancient settlement. From 1961 to 1968, the Ingstads carried out a series of archeological excavations, where they discovered the remains of eight buildings and perhaps a ninth. Their discovery was groundbreaking, as it was the first solid proof of the Vikings visiting America. The houses they discovered were made from sod and peat and displayed similarities with structures in Greenland and Iceland from the period of Norse exploration. Subsequent radiocarbon dating determined that most of the finds at the site can be dated to between AD 1000 and 1020 when the Greenlanders' explorations supposedly took place.

The L'Anse aux Meadows site may be the described Leif Erikson's camp used by the subsequent expeditions. True to that, the excavations revealed the place to be a likely Norse boat repair station, with enough buildings to support between 30 and 160 individuals. The site had two workshops, one with a smithy and the other with a wood workshop, longhouses, and various buildings. It was a Norse station for boat repairing, as there were no signs of animal husbandry or agriculture. Several of the items discovered there are of clear Norse origins. These items include remnants of iron slag from smithing, a bronze pin, animal bones, iron boat rivets, and others. The rivets are indicative of boat repair, as suspected. It is possible that from here, the Norse sailed to the south and entered the Gulf of St. Lawrence, whose coasts are marked with dense green forests and white rocky beaches, as described by the Norse explorers.

One exciting find at the site was the remains of butternuts. Butternuts do not grow in Newfoundland but can be found only as far north as Quebec and then further south. This could indicate that the

Norsemen sailed along the St. Lawrence River and across Lake Ontario, making their explorations there. Several finds across this region could indicate Norse origins, but many were written off as hoaxes or are not positively confirmed. A Viking spear point was found on the southern shores of Ontario Lake in modern New York. Other items found in Ontario and across the waterways of this area have not been confirmed as authentic but could indicate that the Norse explored from Newfoundland much further than is first believed.

Either way, this remains somewhat of a mystery to us. We can only imagine how far the Norsemen sailed in North America and what wonders they discovered or left behind. Perhaps a new discovery is waiting to be made, one that will completely change the story of Viking activity in the New World. We can only marvel at the persevering nature of these Norsemen, whose sails led them to the very ends of the earth. Sadly, however, "Vinland," which seemed promising to them, turned out too hostile and was never settled. What would the world look like today if the Norse did make a colony there? We can only wonder...

Chapter VII: The History of the Viking Longships

Most of the achievements that the Vikings made would not be possible without a few "tricks up the sleeve". Indeed, we cannot write about the Vikings without mentioning one of their most outstanding achievements and best inventions, the famed longship. We all heard tales of dragon-headed ships appearing from the mist and landing on faraway unknown shores laden with fierce Norse warriors ready to face the unknown enemy. The longship was the tool to do this. It was the means of transportation that could propel the Norse across vast oceans. The longship was not invented overnight. There were centuries of ship development in Scandinavia before the Viking Age. Since the ships became so iconic in that period, it goes without saying to write about them in detail. After all, they are a true marvel of ancient technology.

We know that the overall design of the longship is iconic for Scandinavia and is varied in type. Thanks to these variations and their usefulness, the design survived from the earliest medieval period to the Middle Ages. Flexible, slender, and designed with a purpose, these vessels were the finest of their kind. That is what gave the edge to the Norse. The ships display a high level of craftsmanship. You can almost look in disbelief at the attention to detail and advanced building techniques. The ships were "clinker built," meaning they were made with overlapping planks that were riveted together, usually with iron rivets and nails. The ships were symmetrical and had a proper keel alongside other classic ship elements. Of course, we have to mention the famed dragon heads. Longships were often decorated with monstrous heads and shapes at the bow and stern (front and back), used to frighten the enemies, bolster the morale, display marks of ownership, or any other effect. Some also had weathervanes in these spots, which were quite helpful at sea due to the direction of the wind.

It is important to remember that Norse ships were not exclusively war vessels. The types varied between those used for military and trade purposes and those for exploration and setting up new colonies. The trade-oriented ships were broader and deeper and could hold substantial cargo and men. The warships resembled "war canoes." They were slender, narrow, and contained only the rowers, who were also the warriors.

Before the onset of the Viking Age, when traveling on the open oceans was not common, most ships were narrow and light. Sea lanes across Scandinavia thus followed coastal waters. As the Norse contacts spread, they adopted new designs. They adopted the wide-bellied "lodja" ship from the Slavs, which was ideal for trade and cargo transport. These ships varied in design and were seen and recognized from Iceland, Greenland, Newfoundland, the British Isles, the Mediterranean, the Black and Caspian Seas, and even Africa. Everyone knew of the infamous longships. Would you believe it if we said that these ships traveled on land too? This was just one in the extensive list of advantages that the longships had - they were very lightweight, and the Norse warriors could utilize portages, overland routes over which the boats could be rolled or carried to shorten trips. Portages were common in the eastern lands of the Slavs, as well as in Denmark's Jutland peninsula, where Vikings preferred the portage to enter the Baltic Sea rather than sail the long route.

The following is a little bit about the history of the longship. Centuries before the Viking Age began, the Bronze Age people inhabiting Scandinavia were master seafarers. At first, navigation was reserved for rivers, lakes, and coastlines. As the ship designs improved, longer routes could be taken across gulfs and open seas. Of course, the oceans were not braved. One of the earliest known longship designs is the "Hjortspring" boat. Resembling a very slender and narrow canoe, this boat is markedly different from the latter described longship but provides a good insight into the evolution of the design. The

Hjortspring boat was discovered in a peat bog, and was built around 400 BC, when it was deposited as a sacrificial offering. It is almost identical to ships displayed on petroglyphs (rock carvings dated to the Nordic Bronze Age). This, as well as the high level of craftsmanship, tells us that the boat design is much older than the boat itself, and that the tradition spans thousands of years. The boat could house a crew of 20 rowers, and weighed just 530 kilograms (1,168 lbs), which means that it could have been easily carried over land. Without a doubt, the tribe with such a warship had a clear advantage over their enemies. The basics of such a design persisted over the centuries and were refined until the beginning of the Viking Age. By this time, its importance as the centerpiece of Norse culture was deeply rooted in the people's consciousness. It was both a functional item and a symbol, both religious and material.

Of course, Scandinavians required ships; that is the simplest explanation. Their lands are primarily forested and mountainous, with plenty of natural ports and easy access to the sea. Maritime trade routes were thus a logical solution, and the evolution of shipbuilding was a natural development. During the Nordic Stone Age and the latter Bronze Age, the most valuable ships also had a religious symbolism. They were sacrificed as ceremonial and votive offerings, with weapons and other items of importance. By the time of the Viking Age, pragmatism had taken over, as the Norse depended on their trading ports and the North and Baltic Seas for their survival and prosperity. Even then, a ceremonial role persisted, especially in lavish ship burials, which we will write about later. Through this cultural, religious, and practical importance, the Viking ship design became one of the most powerful and important vessels in early medieval Europe.

It is fascinating to know that the Viking ship was not "standardized." The individual vessels often varied from maker to maker and region to region. Depending on the area and the regional forests, different woods were also used, and some makers implemented their own distinct details. For example, Danish ships were usually made from oak, but Swedish and Norwegian ones were made from pine. Minor adjustments were made depending on the area used, and the waters sailed. Here we need to make an important note. Although often called "warships," these vessels are best described as troop transports. The longship had no "armament" of its own. It was best suited for traveling at high speeds, outrunning and outmaneuvering enemies, and quickly delivering a battle-ready band of warriors to almost any shore. Examples where a longship was used as a "battle tool" are recorded in the 10th century, when several longships were tied together, thus forming an efficient platform for infantry warfare. These events were rare, and the true power of the longship lay in its speed and nimbleness. It was ideal for navigating European rivers, both narrow and shallow. When assembled in large fleets, the ships were a true terror for the enemy. For example, in the ninth century, the Norsemen sailed immense fleets into the weakened Frankish empire, which they assaulted through its navigable rivers, such as the Seine. In AD 841, these fleets sacked Rouen, Quentovic in AD 842, and Hamburg in AD 845. The fleet had as many as 600 longships, a massive army. They became the symbol of plunder, terror, and bloodshed, and enemies quaked when witnessing them. They also called them "dragon ships," mainly due to the stylized dragon heads displayed on the prow. The Franks notably called them "drakuskippan," meaning dragon ships. The Franks and the Anglo-Saxons had difficulty countering these "dragon ships" simply because they were too advanced for their time - a clear result of many centuries of shipbuilding traditions.

There were several distinct types of ships used by the Vikings, each with its own advantages and specialties. Not all were designed for war. A typical cargo ship used for transporting goods and trading was the so-called "knarr." It had an average length of roughly 16 meters (54 feet), and its broad and deep hull could carry as much as 24 tons, a substantial weight for the time. The Slavs, living close to the Baltic

Sea, primarily influenced this design. For centuries, the Norse had a cultural exchange (as well as conflict) with the Slavs, who were also masters of navigating rivers. These two cultures influenced each other, and the cargo ship was, in many aspects, derived from an earlier Slavic design. The exchange of ideas was particularly accentuated in the 900s, when King Harald Bluetooth allied with the Baltic Slavs, chiefly the Obodrites. Some say that without the cargo ship design, the Vikings couldn't have launched successive invasions of Britain and hauled enough resources and men for settlement. The knarr was a sturdy and stout boat and was much heavier than the classic longship. This meant that they depended mainly on their sails and the wind. The oars were used only as auxiliary power.

All this made the knarr ideal for long voyages on the open sea or the oceans. For example, Bjarni Herjolfsson, the first Norseman to sight North America, sailed there in a knarr. Modern research suggests that this type of ship could cross the distance of 121 kilometers (75 miles) in a single day and had a crew of 20 to 30 men. In time, the knarr was the routine vessel used to cross the North Atlantic, carrying livestock, people, and goods without issue, reaching Greenland, Iceland, and elsewhere. It was so efficient that its overall design survived well after the Viking Age, later influencing the development of the trading cog, widely used by the merchants of the Hanseatic League.

On the other hand, the longship was graceful, slim, long, light, and narrow - the perfect speed boat. The average speed of a longship would vary, but a reasonable estimate is between 5 to 10 knots at the lowest (9 to 19 kilometers per hour) and 15 knots (28 kilometers per hour) at best. Taking the latter estimate, we can deduce that a Viking longship, under suitable conditions, could cross 672 kilometers in 24 hours. These ships were easy to maneuver and had very shallow drafts, which meant they were fast but could also sail in water only one meter deep. That also meant that they allowed for beach landing (the classic method of Viking disembarkment) and that they were exceptionally light - which allowed carrying over land. One fantastic feature of the longship is impressive and highlights the ingenuity of the ancient Norsemen. Because the ship was symmetrical or "double-ended," they could quickly reverse their direction without turning around. Row in the other direction, and you are suddenly going backward at the same speed! Of course, the speed of the longboat depended not only on the winds and the sails but also on the oars. The entire length of the boat displayed oars manned by rowers, with the largest ships having 34 rowing positions. Together with the sail, the oars gave it great speed.

Being so significant and widespread, the longships had their variations, too. The designs that the Vikings called "snekkja" (or snekke), meaning "snake," were sleek and narrow and usually the smallest longships deployed. They usually had 20 rowing benches and a length of 17 meters (56 feet). Its crew would number 41 men. All this means that the snekkja was one of the most common ships in Scandinavia. Famous legends state that in AD 1028, King Canute the Great used a massive fleet of 1,200 snekkja ships in Norway. One significant advantage of this lightweight design is that it did not require a port - the ship could be beached wherever it was suitable. The design was so efficient that it survived into modern times, where it is still called snekke in Norway.

The skeid (skeið), meaning "slider" or " speeder," is another type of longship. The skeid was more extensive and more potent warships, having 30 rowing benches at least. Some of the largest Viking longships ever discovered belong to this design. A discovery was made in the Danish harbor of Roskilde, when archeologists found a group of Viking ships that were sunk. Each was made in a different place (as far away as Dublin in Ireland), and they all belong to the skeid type. One of these is the longest Viking ship ever discovered - it measures 37 meters (121 feet) and was made in AD 1025.

Perhaps the most famous type of longship was the so-called "drakkar," or "dreki," meaning "dragon." It sported more than 30 rowing benches and was prized by expert raiders and plunderers - the real Vikings. The owners of these dragon ships often had them elaborately decorated - they were slender, elegant, and most unusual in their appearance. The name "dragonship" likely came from these ships, as their prows were decorated with heads of menacing beasts meant to instill terror in the enemies. These ships are today known only from historical sources and mentions, such as the Norse sagas. The earliest mention of a "Drakkar" is dated to the 10th century when King Harald Fairhair was said to own one. However, the first drakkar whose size was also mentioned belonged to the famed Olav Tryggvason. First mentioned was a ship with 30 rowing seats built in Nidaros in AD 995, called "Tranin". He later owns the even longer, 34-rowing seats "Ormrinn Langi" (The Long Serpent), built in the winter between AD 999 and 1000. From this, we can realize that the dragon ship was the most prized of all Viking warships, highly influential and owned only by the most famous of Viking raiders.

What did it take to build such an exquisite vessel? Even more importantly, how did the Norsemen navigate it across the vastness of the oceans? For decades researchers attempted to answer these questions and were helped in no small part by archeology. As far as shipbuilding went, archeology was vital for understanding the process. Around the time when the Vikings expanded into Dublin in Ireland and Jorvik in England, between AD 875 and 954, the development of the longship reached its absolute peak. Around this time, in AD 890, one of the best Norse ships ever discovered was built, the Gokstad Ship.

Some of the finds from the archaeological excavations in the Coppergate area of York, in England, included a set of well-preserved Viking woodworking tools. In this kit were discovered the essential tools needed for building a longship. The find gave significant insight into Viking shipbuilding. Archaeologists found that the Viking woodworker had a full arsenal of sophisticated tools. Also discovered was a set of sharpening stones from Norway because the tools always needed to be sharp. Next, the craftsman would need an adequate wood supply before the building can begin. Some current estimates suggest that it could have taken a small team of Viking craftsmen up to 28,000 work hours to complete a large longship. This was, however, estimated based on a modern team of workers who recreated a ship in four years. A more reasonable estimate for the Viking Age would be as low as seven months to complete a boat. Either way, it was undoubtedly painstaking and detailed work that required immense knowledge. We can only imagine how vital shipbuilders were in Viking society.

Still, building a longship can be seen as one art form, but sailing it was another affair. Even with good winds, filled sails, and all oars manned, the matter of navigation remained. For the ancient Vikings, this was one of the major obstacles to overcome. That is why they initially stayed in the waters of Scandinavia before eventually sailing across the ocean. As they learned to navigate open waters, the Vikings became the dominant seafarers of the North Atlantic and beyond. You may ask, how did they do it?

Historians agree that the Vikings were experts in judging wind direction and speed of movement and understood the currents and the high and low tides. However, the techniques they used for navigation still need to be thoroughly understood. Scholars, however, agree that they likely used the stars for plotting their course and had some "sort of primitive astrolabe," an ancient astronomical instrument. One similar device was discovered during an excavation of a Viking farm in southern Greenland, one of the remotest areas that the Norse inhabited. Found was a part of a circular wooden disk that had unique carvings on it. It was termed the "Viking Sundial" and confirmed a hypothesis that it was a primitive sun compass. Soon after, also in Greenland, a stone version was discovered. Both had straight and hyperbolic carvings, indicating the solstices, and could allow the Vikings to cross the seas along latitude 61° North. These compasses were small enough to be held flat in one's palm.

Since the discovery, the sun compass was reconstructed and utilized, showing in detail how the Norse could ingeniously rely on the sun and the shadows to determine the position of the true north and thus navigate the waters. The navigator would observe the place where the shadow fell on the disc and was, therefore, able to sail along a line of latitude. A similar discovery at Wolin in 2000, near the shores of the Baltic Sea, further confirmed the theory of sun compass use. This is just another indication of how advanced the Vikings were, not simple raiders as history portrays them. Modern sailing teams used the Viking sun compass in 1984 during a reenactment of a longship voyage across the North Atlantic. The compass worked brilliantly and was very accurate, to within $\pm 5°$.

This wasn't all the Norse navigators had in their sea-faring arsenal. The Norse sagas mention unique "sunstones" for observing the sun even in cloudy conditions. It was theorized that these sunstones, or "Iceland spar," are natural crystals capable of polarizing the sun's light. It was ideal for navigating during daylight hours. Today we know them as optical calcite or silfurberg. As this crystal changes color, it would allow the Norsemen to determine the sun's position or azimuth, even if the day is overcast. Since the stone uses light polarization, it works best when the sun hangs at lower altitudes, closer to the horizon. This makes perfect sense, as Norsemen traveled extensively near the polar regions, where the sun is close to the horizon for most of the year. The sagas mention these sunstones on multiple occasions.

"The King looked about and saw no blue sky...then the King took the Sunstone and held it up, and then he saw where the Sun beamed from the stone" (Hrafns saga Sveinbjarnarsonar)

Olaf grabbed a Sunstone, looked at the sky and saw from where the light came, from which he guessed the position of the invisible Sun" (St. Olaf's Saga)

Historical records and sagas also mention some notable Viking navigators that helped future generations. One of the earliest we know of was Almgren, who describes a method of navigation as such:

"All the measurements of angles were made with what was called a 'half wheel' (a kind of half sun-diameter which corresponds to about sixteen minutes of arc). This was something that was known to every skipper at that time, or to the long-voyage pilot or kendtmand ('man who knows the way') who sometimes went along on voyages ... When the sun was in the sky, it was not, therefore, difficult to find the four points of the compass, and determining latitude did not cause any problems either."

There is a Viking navigator named Stjerner Oddi (Oddi of the Stars) who compiled a unique chart that showed the direction of sunrise and sunset and thus enabled navigators to sail their longships across great distances with relative ease. Lastly, as we discussed earlier in this book, birds were another useful navigation tool the Vikings used. Viking mariners would take caged ravens on long-distance or exploratory journeys. If the land was not visible, they would release the bird, which instinctively flies for land. This would then give them a new course to follow. We can see that the Norse had a variety of methods for navigation at their disposal. Combining them all or utilizing selected ones helped them reach their destinations accurately.

From modern research, we know that the Vikings were thinking about everything, especially when sailing on long journeys. In the end, if we consider all that we know about the famed Viking longship, we can understand that it was the most advanced vessel of its time. That is why the Vikings spread like wildfire through Europe, colonizing a number of new places in only a few hundred years. Of course, their shipbuilding methods greatly impacted other civilizations they met. Many European nations borrowed heavily from the longship design, even after the Viking Age was gone. In Scandinavia, the longship design remained the dominant military vessel for a long while after the Vikings were gone. However, by the 14th century, they began to display disadvantages against new and modern ships that appeared in Europe. They were now low and helpless against the tall and wide great ships. Gradually, they went out of use and out of memory. The last Viking longship was defeated in AD 1429.

The Viking longship was so prized and revered, that it played a central part in the burial of prominent Viking chieftains, raiders, and kings. Both men and women of prominence and renown would receive the privilege of a "ship burial." Sometimes, the ship was used as a funeral pyre, and burned together with the deceased. Sometimes it was buried entirely under a mound. From the latter cases we know of famed longships that the archeologists succeeded in excavating. In a lavish ceremony, the deceased individual was placed onto a ship, and accompanied by many exquisite and prized possessions. These, alongside the sacrificed animals and slaves, were meant to serve the deceased in the otherworld. The custom was spread across the Norse world, and many ship burials were excavated, revealing ships such as the Oseberg, Gokstad, Ladby, and other ships. There could have been humbler ship burials, where the deceased was placed on a smaller boat in the same fashion, launched onto the water, and then shot with flaming arrows, where both the ship and the deceased would disappear in flames. The tradition reaches far back in time, perhaps as early as the Nordic Stone Age, as evidenced by the sacrificial Nydam boat discovered in Denmark.

The ship burial custom spread wherever the Vikings ventured. In their new realm amongst the Slavs, in the land of the Rus', the Norse custom gained an even deeper, more lavish ceremony that was meant to depart the deceased into the otherworld in high style. The Muslim traveler, Ibn Fadlan, visited the Norsemen in the lands of the Rus', and left a striking account of their funeral ceremony. It is one of the foremost contemporary accounts that we have on the Viking ship burial.

"The dead chieftain was put in a temporary grave which was covered for ten days until they had sewn new clothes for him. One of his thrall women volunteered to join him in the afterlife and she was guarded day and night, being given a great amount of intoxicating drinks while she sang happily. When the time had arrived for cremation, they pulled his longship ashore and put it on a platform of wood, and they made a bed for the dead chieftain on the ship. Thereafter, an old woman referred to as the "Angel of Death" put cushions on the bed. She was responsible for the ritual. Then they disinterred the chieftain and gave him new clothes. In his grave, he received intoxicating drinks, fruits and a stringed instrument. The chieftain was put into his bed with all his weapons and grave offerings around him. Then they had two horses run themselves sweaty, cut them to pieces, and threw the meat into the ship. Finally, they sacrificed a hen and a cock.

Meanwhile, the thrall girl went from one tent to the other and had sexual intercourse with the men. Every man told her "tell your master that I did this because of my love for him". While in the afternoon, they moved the thrall girl to something that looked like a door frame, where she was lifted on the palms of the men three times. Every time, the girl told of what she saw. The first time, she saw her father and mother, the second time, she saw all her relatives, and the third time she saw her master in the afterworld. There, it was green and beautiful and together with him, she saw men and young boys. She saw that her master beckoned for her. By using intoxicating drinks, they thought to put the thrall girl in an ecstatic trance that made her psychic and through the symbolic action with the door frame, she would then see into the realm of the dead.

The same ritual also appears in the Icelandic short story Völsa þáttr, where two pagan Norwegian men lift the lady of the household over a door frame to help her look into the otherworld.

Thereafter, the thrall girl was taken away to the ship. She removed her bracelets and gave them to the old woman. Thereafter she removed her finger rings and gave them to the old woman's daughters, who had guarded her. Then they took her aboard the ship, but they did not allow her to enter the tent where the dead chieftain lay. The girl received several vessels of intoxicating drinks, and she sang and bade her friends farewell. Then the girl was pulled into the tent and the men started to beat on the shields so her screams could not be heard. Six men entered into the tent to have intercourse with the girl, after which they put her onto her master's bed. Two men grabbed her hands and two men her wrists. The angel of death put a rope around her neck and while two men pulled the rope, the old woman stabbed the girl between her ribs with a knife. Thereafter, the relatives of the dead chieftain arrived with a burning torch and set the ship aflame. It is said that the fire facilitates the voyage to the realm of the dead, but unfortunately, the account does not tell to which realm the deceased was to go. Afterwards, a round barrow was built over the ashes and in the center of the mound they erected a staff of birch wood, where they carved the names of the dead chieftain and his king. Then they departed in their ships."

It was a grim custom, without a doubt, as gloomy as were many aspects of the Viking world. Once paired with the equally grim worldview of the ancient Slavs, the funerary ship burial custom gained a much darker aspect, such as you have just read above. Alas, such was the ancient world in which the Norsemen reigned with fire and sword, blood and terror, opportunism and injustice. It was a word where the strong ruled, where the ax and the sword carved out a world fit for one group, and one group only - the Vikings.

Conclusion

In this book, we touched upon many essential topics for the history of the Vikings. We focused on their origins and traditions, their sudden appearance in Europe and their ongoing conflict with the Anglo-Saxons in England. We talked of their expeditions in the east, their contacts with the Slavs and the emergence of the distinct Rus' culture. We also focused on their explorations and the establishments and fates of colonies such as the Faroe Islands, Iceland, Greenland, and Vinland. We showed a side of the Viking character that is not all about pillage and invasion but about exploration and colonization. We also mentioned the famous Viking ship, the one thing without which the Norsemen could not accomplish any of the things we just listed. Even with all this, you would be wrong to think that the story ends here. No, we just scratched the surface and will pick this tale up in our follow-up book, where we will write of the Vikings in Ireland, the Isle of Man, Normandy, Iberia, North Africa and the Mediterranean. The Norsemen traveled far and wide and left a wealth of stories and adventures to be recounted for posterity. After all, what was a Viking if not far-traveled and battle-scarred?

For several centuries, the defiant Vikings determined the fate of Europe's Kingdoms, their sails recognizable from the ice of Greenland to the sands of the Caspian Sea. Their tale deserves our admiration and its rightful place in our world's history. Above all, it deserves at least another book that promises even more exciting stories than the first one!

Keep an eye out for our second book on the Vikings, as we meet the Viking descendants in France, the Normans, and the extravagant Byzantine Royal protectors, the Varangian Guard. We will write of the Vikings' endurance and their failures, too, of their illustrious religion and far-reaching traditions. We will also talk of their fate. Just as we began this book with their origins, we will finish the next one with their eventual demise and disappearance.

By Aleksa Vučković

References:

Bruun, P. 1997. *The Viking Ship*. Journal of Coastal Research, 4.

Brøgger, A. W. 1951. *The Viking ships, their ancestry and evolution.* Dreyer.

Evans, A. 2008. *Iceland: The Bradt Travel Guide.* Bradt Travel Guides.

Esposito, G. 2021. *Armies of the Vikings, AD 793–1066: History, Organization and Equipment.* Pen and Sword Military.

Greenling, J. 2016. *The Technology of the Vikings.* Cavendish Square Publishing.

Hall, R. 2010. *Viking Age Archaeology.* Shire Publications

Hall, R. 2012. *Exploring the World of the Vikings.* Thames & Hudson.

Hinds, K. 2010. *Vikings.* Marshall Cavendish.

Hjardar, K. 2018. *Vikings.* The Rosen Publishing Group, Inc.

Jóhannesson, J. 2014. *A History of the Old Icelandic Commonwealth: Islendinga Saga.* University of Manitoba Press.

Jones, G. 2001. *A History of the Vikings.* Oxford University Press.

Kendrick, T. D. 2012. *A History of the Vikings.* Courier Corporation.

Mark, J. 2019. *The Legendary Settlement Of Iceland.* Ancient History Encyclopedia. [Online] Available at: https://www.ancient.eu/article/1317/the-legendary-settlement-of-iceland/

Various. 2005. *Viking Empires.* Cambridge University Press.

Don't miss out!

Visit the website below and you can sign up to receive emails whenever History Nerds publishes a new book. There's no charge and no obligation.

https://books2read.com/r/B-A-ODOK-UJMCC

Connecting independent readers to independent writers.